Awakening

How a 53 year old wife and mother "became" a lesbian.

Jo Jom —
Thanks so much !
Pat Stone
6 - 8 · 09

Pat Stone

ISBN: 1-4392-2197-9
ISBN-13: 9781439221976

Visit www.booksurge.com to order additional copies.

Dedicated to Mother (Mema)
For your unconditional love.

"And the day came when the risk to remain tight in a bud was more painful than the risk to blossom."

Anis Nin

Preface

I want to have a conversation with you; and by telling you my true story, I hope to be instrumental in sending a message of courage, honesty, and integrity – with a little humor in the mix. Most of us, at one time or another, must face what may seem to be an overwhelming obstacle, perhaps a life changing event. Our decisions at that time do not always make everyone around us happy, but we do the best we can. My story is one of self discovery and getting a second chance at life, while still cherishing many aspects of the past.

As you will see, I have the challenge of sharing my personal story and perhaps reaching others in a similar situation, without infringing on my ex husband's privacy. I tried very hard to be sensitive in that regard – sensitive to him, as well as to others whose lives touched mine.

Of course, as in all memoirs, the comments made here are from my perspective. However, my point of view is greatly substantiated by the numerous notes, letters, and articles that I kept from that era. Please come along with me on this journey of discovery.

Chapter 1

It was Tuesday, October 29, 1996, the day I planned to tell my husband. I sat in the den of my comfortable home in Dallas, Texas, about to cause a major change in my family and in my life. How could this have happened?

We had been married for 35 years, and we had two grown children. Dan had been a wonderful provider, a good friend and confidant, and a dedicated father. I had known him since I was 15 years old. We were engaged when I was 16; we married June 18, 1961, when I was 18, and he was 21. We met at Wesley Methodist Church in Wichita Falls, Texas.

Was I about to lose a good friend? No, I was sure he would understand and be supportive. I was confident that he had been a faithful husband over those many years; he was (is) of high moral fiber and unquestionable ethics. I felt certain that with time, he and I would continue our friendship, go to movies, have dinner, and share holidays and other occasions with our children. He would understand that none of this was his fault. Was I being naive?

How does a 53 year old wife tell her 57 year old husband that she now sees herself as lesbian? Would he be shocked? I didn't want to hurt him. I wanted him to realize that this was an orientation issue for me, not a rejection of him. Was that too much to ask? Perhaps. Surely he would admire me for being honest with him, and especially for never having cheated on him. Man, I had not even acted on this new discovery, not a kiss, not a date – nothing.

Honesty has always played a big part in my life. It was ingrained in me by my dad.

He had his faults, but he admired honesty and demanded it. In fact, the only real spanking he gave me was centered around this topic; I was around six years old. That winter evening had started our perfectly. The clear Texas sky twinkled with brilliant stars. I sat in the front seat of our Chevy between Mama and Daddy as we drove down the country road to Wichita Falls to see a movie. Actually, when I was a child in the 1950s the term was *show*, as in *The Last Picture Show* that was filmed near Wichita Falls in 1971.

I felt safe as I watched Daddy's strong hands grip the wheel as our car bumped along the dry ruts in the road. This excursion was rare for us. It was a thirty minute trip from our farm to town, and it meant coming home late, a difficulty for my parents. My dad had to get up early in the mornings to milk our cows, and my mom usually had the early shift at the bakery.

However, there we were, going to a show like a real family. I was so excited. Nothing made me happier than the three of us doing something fun together. As I sat between my parents, my legs dangled over the seat. I could not keep them still because of the excitement. As I jiggled my legs my dress came up above my knees, and my mom saw a Band-Aid on my upper leg.

Mama said, "Patsy, I thought I told you to stay out of the Band-Aids." "I did," I replied, not realizing that she knew otherwise. Earlier in the day, Mama caught me standing on a kitchen chair, getting the Band-Aids out of the kitchen cabinet, and putting them on my arms. She told me to take them off, put the tin back in the cabinet, and to stay out of them. I still do not understand the fascination I had with those Band-Aids, but they kept calling my name and asking me to play with them. I decided just one on my leg would be perfect.

Daddy quickly realized what had happened, that I had told a lie - saying that I had not bothered the Band-Aids again; and there was blatant proof of my lie stuck to my leg. It was obvious that he was disappointed in me. He did not yell; he didn't have to because a lecture from him in his serious tone of voice was always scary to me.

He explained to me the seriousness of lying, that I should never lie; and to show me the importance of telling the truth, he said that he must give me a spanking when we got home from the show. We drove along in total silence. Then his stern but compassionate voice said, "Patsy, I want you to enjoy the show, so I'm going to pull over and get this over with right now."

He turned the car into a little side road and told me to get out. It was very dark and cold outside. I didn't know what to expect as I followed Mama out of the car. I walked around the front of the car, through the headlights, and stood in front of my dad. He told me to turn around as he took off his belt and spanked me several times. It didn't hurt physically, perhaps because he did not make me take off my little coat, and I don't think he hit me very hard. I was aware even then that this was something he didn't want to do, but something he felt he had to do. Honesty was very important to him, and after that night, it became a part of me as well.

So it never occurred to me to be less than honest with Dan. At least I knew that he would not think less of me for being gay (I use the words *lesbian* and *gay* interchangeably). He was understanding of this issue for many reasons, mainly because our daughter, T.J., came out as lesbian seven years prior. I know; that's rather unusual, isn't it? I think when a parent has a gay or lesbian child, that parent often looks at herself and asks: "Could I also be gay?" I did ask myself that question seven years ago, and I didn't see the signs. I remember even saying to my daughter, "I could see that women as they get older might want to live together for companionship, but I don't get the sex part." However, after developing a crush on a woman, I could certainly understand the sexual connection.

I do recall making vague comments during my marriage regarding the relationships between men and women such as: "It *must* be a biological thing for men and women to be together because why would it happen; they don't get along; they are so different; the women end up in one area at a party and the men in the other, etc." I often said that if something happened to Dan, I would *never* marry again. Did these comments mean anything or were they common reactions of both straight and gay women?

When I looked back at my life, I saw a few signs. However, I came from an era when women were expected to marry and have a family right away, and I had never even heard the word "lesbian" when I married in 1961. I had heard of homosexual men, but didn't realize that could apply to women as well. So what did I know about my orientation? All I knew was that I wanted to marry a man (of course) who would be kind and non violent, someone who would be a good father. My dad had been violent toward my mom, as had my grandfather (his dad) to my grandmother. My main goal even at that early age was to not let that happen to me.

Dan fit that description of a kind man, a non violent man. He was persistent regarding our getting married; my friends were getting married so I said "yes." I was only 16, but we planned to wait two years for marriage – after I finished high school and he finished college (We did wait). I told him at the time that I wouldn't be very "demonstrative," and he said he understood. I think we both believed that was due to how I was raised, the lack of affection shown by my parents, my dad's over bearing attitude, etc. Now I wonder…

I will always remember an evening that Dan and I walked into his parent's living room and saw them watching television; his mom was lying on the couch with her head in his dad's lap. I was stunned at this show of affection. I felt ill at ease, but touched by the scene. I had never witnessed such a thing in my family.

I sensed that my parents loved one another, but I rarely saw any obvious signs of such feelings. The closest thing to that was when I heard my dad apologizing to my mom after a fight, telling her that "it would never happen again." Oh how I wanted to believe that. I wanted to be part of a "perfect family," and there were times I had that feeling, at least for a moment. I so loved the few times the three of us played softball by the side of our old farmhouse. Daddy would hit the ball to Mother and me; we would catch it, getting a certain score for fly balls and skinners. I was in heaven! I so wanted that feeling to last, but I knew that there would soon be a time when that glorious, secret feeling of being part of a happy family would be shattered. It was only a matter of time before the other shoe would drop.

My dad was a handsome and intelligent man; he was very kind most of the time. However, from out of no where he would fly into a rage at my mom, usually due to what he considered a mistake made by her. I often lay in bed, my stomach hurting and in knots, listening to him berating her. One of the scariest incidents happened one afternoon after Mama and I returned from Wichita Falls to our dairy farm. Daddy had sent us there to pick up some medicine for the cows. We drove up into the fields to give the medicine to my dad as he was plowing. I sat in the car as Mama got out, leaving her door open as she took the package to him.

He stepped down from the tractor, took the medicine and saw that she had gotten the wrong type of drug. He suddenly began yelling at her, struggling with her, and hitting her in the face. I heard him say, "Honey, someday I'm going to kill you." She ran back and got in the car with me, and we started to drive off. He jumped on the hood of the car, trying to stop her. I saw his eyes through the windshield, and they were cold and scary.

We managed to drive away as he tumbled off the car. As we passed by the house, Mama said that she was going to leave and get a divorce. I will never forget to this day my words of: "No, I want both of you." How could a child (I must have been around seven) say such a thing after witnessing such violence? Guess it shows how much a child will sometimes put up with in order to have both parents. I still have regrets and guilt about being afraid to stand up to my dad; however, I knew if I did, it would have been my mom who would have paid the price.

Mama didn't go for a divorce, but drove to the farm of my grandparents, Daddy's parents, which was about 30 minutes away. Grannie was very sympathetic and said they should call the police. The police was not called; instead, Grannie doctored Mama's bruised face. Papa said nothing; he was known to have given Grannie bruises over the years so he had no room to talk. Later Daddy came to take us home, full of apologies and promises to "never do it again."

There were several incidents similar to this like the time Daddy became furious when Mama dropped one side of the tow sack she was holding as he was pouring feed into it with a shovel. He hit her hard on the leg with that shovel, leaving a huge bruise. What makes a man do something like that? Does he hate women? Does he hate himself? I never figured it out, and I don't think there is a logical answer. He never had outbursts like that with other people, only with her.

It's a miracle that I did not think that all men were like my dad and grandfather. My aunt (sister of my dad and daughter of Grannie and Papa), who was only 10 years older than I, had a boyfriend (who she later married) who was so kind and gentle to her. From seeing that relationship, I realized that all men were not like my dad. That insight made me determined to find a man who was kind and non violent. A therapist later told me that it was very unusual that I had been so determined to break that chain of violence.

When I was eleven years old, my dad's rages seemed to lessen after we moved from the farm to Wichita Falls. Perhaps he had been frustrated with trying to be a farmer. The words "dairy farm" may bring to mind a pleasant image, but it was not like that where I lived. That part of north Texas was dry and barren; thorny mesquite trees dotted the land. My mind sees no color within nature when I reflect on those days. I only saw birds sitting on electrical lines, not in lush trees or bushes. My dad was always at the mercy of the weather concerning his crops, and always feared diseases hitting his cows.

We had an outdoor toilet – a wooden outhouse, a "one holer." I had no fear of walking out there during the night, but I was concerned about the spiders that lurked down and around the hole. And that smell – a person never forgets the smell of an outhouse.

Of course, we had the typical cellar near the house. I had heard that some people had cellars that had nice concrete floors and electric lights – not ours. There were rickety wooden steps going down into a dark musty smelling cave with dirt floors, walls and ceiling. There were shelves of old canned goods lined up on one wall, spider webs clinging to the jars. I remember a kerosene lamp with matches sitting on an old wooden table. The sound of rats scattering about was scary.

I dreaded going down into that cellar, and my dad rarely went there. He usually decided to weather the storm in the house, lying on a cot reading a paperback book. However, Mother made me go down there with her several times; she was very afraid of the Texas storms, and the threatening tornados. My dad did join us on one particular stormy night. I will always remember his hanging on to the rope tied to the door of the cellar. It took all his strength to keep the door from blowing open. When we emerged from the cellar, our house was still standing. However, many years later after we had left that farm, the famous Wichita Falls tornado of 1979 completely destroyed the house and all of the barns – everything was flattened.

We did not have the convenience of a phone on our farm. A neighbor had to drive to our place to inform Mother the day her mom died; he had gotten the call from our relatives in California. Nor did we have a television, but I heard that a girl at school had one. It was always referred to as a "television," never a TV. It sounded like a miracle to me - to be able to see moving pictures in your home. Soon my aunt bought one for her and her parents (Grannie and Papa). Every Monday night we drove to their farm to watch "I Love Lucy." One evening my great-grandparents (Papa's parents) joined us. Great-Grannie was sitting next to my dad on the couch. She leaned over to him, pointed at the television and asked, "Do you think they can see us?"

As I mentioned earlier, Daddy became frustrated with the life of a farmer and decided to move to Wichita Falls. He became a police officer, and quickly moved up to the rank of a Lieutenant, then a Detective, and eventually created the first Juvenile Division of the Wichita Falls Police Department. During those days, I only remember an occasional black eye inflicted on my mom – not that I am saying that was a minor thing! My dad's violence was a family secret; from the outside, he appeared to be the pillar of the community. He rarely hit me.

However, one evening when I was around twelve, he asked me to walk to the store to get a package of American cheese slices We always bought Kraft American Cheese with the blue design. By mistake (there's that "mistake" connection), I brought home Kraft Old English slices; it also had a blue design on the package. He had a fit, yelled at me, and slammed the screen door as he went outside.

I started complaining to Mother about his getting so mad. He must have heard me through the screen door because he stormed in, his eyes steely gray, as he took off his belt and told me to *never* talk back to him. I was wearing shorts, and the belt curled around my upper left leg as I fell to the floor, grabbing that leg. Mother rushed to me; Daddy told her to get back or she would get the same.

He knelt down to look at the mark; he then went to the medicine cabinet, got a salve and rubbed it on the wound. I don't remember his apologizing; he may have felt he was in the right because I was never to "talk back." I wasn't able to wear shorts for a long, long time because of the bruise left behind.

Why do I share this side of my dad with you? I know I risk your thinking that this is why I "became" gay. I don't believe that's true at all, especially since I realized early on that all men were not like that. I did not grow up hating or fearing men. I want you to know this information in order to show that perhaps this experience was the reason I did not see my orientation when Dan asked me to marry him. I knew I did not have those romantic feelings I should have had, but I thought it was due to my experience with my dad.

Actually, the reasons I did not have those romantic feelings, the reason I felt I would not be very "demonstrative" was probably because I was gay all along. But who knew, especially in the late fifties in Wichita Falls, Texas. I assumed I was not very affectionate due to the bad example set at home and the fear of my dad, and I hoped things would get better in that area. I would have been up front with Dan if I had know then what I know now. Also, romance is so different than sex; enough said on that point.

I also want to say that I did not have those romantic feelings for other boys either. Even though I became engaged at age 16, I did date several boys before that time. I was not comfortable with that scene. However, in that time of the fifties, it was difficult to know what was unusual from what was expected. For instance, girls were not supposed to really enjoy being sexual.

To jump ahead a little, it is very clear to me that having a difficult father does not cause a girl to "become" gay, using my daughter as an example. T.J. had (still has) a very gentle, lovable, affectionate father. She is a very happy, productive, and well adjusted lesbian.

So what does cause a person to be gay or lesbian? Does the cause really matter? Guess the jury is still out on the cause or causes. I like to think of it as a natural occurring phenomena. It's not the norm, but it is normal. It's sad to me that people are sometimes thought of as "less than" because of who they are attracted to, because of who they love. In the big scheme of things, it's such a minor issue. Attitudes regarding this have changed so much over the recent years; there is much more understanding in this area now. I do wonder if there is sometimes a genetic or biological link in some families.

I continued to look back at my childhood to see if I had missed some signs of my orientation. As a young child, I disliked all dolls except a "boy doll" that I loved to walk (drag around by my side); I held his hand with my right hand, while my left hand was in my jean pant pocket, jingling my coins – just like my Daddy. I won't even try to analyze that. My mom so wanted me to love dolls. She often told me the story of when she gave me one to play with, and I said, "But it's not real." I saw dolls as a mockery, because I wanted a baby brother or baby sister so badly. I was very maternal, but I wanted the real thing. My daughter, T.J., loved dolls as a child, all types and sizes. Go figure.

As an older child on the farm, I was a *Tomboy*, (what a weird term) as were many farm girls. I usually dressed in jeans, and on the playground I looked with disfavor on the "girlie girls" who jumped rope, played jacks, and chatted. I loved to play softball with the boys, along with other girls. I continued playing softball when I moved to McGaha Elementary in Wichita Falls. However, at that school we girls were not allowed to play ball with the boys. The principal said if we could hit the ball far enough to break one of our school windows, we could play with the boys. I'm sure he knew we would never be able to do that.

I'm not sure that my ball playing meant anything regarding orientation. I feel that for some girls, it might mean something; for others, it might not. I did not continue playing ball after elementary school. During my junior high school years, I began to shed the jeans and became feminine in my way of dressing. Was I beginning to follow society's rules as to what was proper for girls? I don't know.

As I am sure you are aware, there are lesbians who appear very "traditionally feminine" in appearance, and there are lesbians who appear more "butch" in appearance, and there are lesbians who appear somewhere in the middle. It sounds silly to even be concerned about this; however, many of us who come out later in life do look back to see if there were early signs (even if we are not sure what the signs would be).

As I continued to look back, one thing that stood out was a very good friend I had in seventh grade named "Carol." I met her at McGaha Elementary in Wichita Falls. I know it is common for little girls to have crushes on their friends and to be very close to them. However, as I looked back at her, I realized that I saw her differently than any of my other girlfriends. I always realized how nice her lips were, her short (unusual for that time) curly hair, the way her eyebrows curved. I remembered my mom reading a note I had gotten from Carol; she read it, but said nothing. I then realized that the note sounded like a note written to a girl from a boy. Those were the only words I had for it, and I am surprised I picked up on that. Carol moved away from Wichita Falls shortly after that, so I don't know if anything would have become more obvious in time. Or did it mean nothing?

In high school I had little time to become interested in boys since I was engaged at such an early age. I no longer played soft ball, but I had a wicked side arm volleyball serve! After marriage I was in college, but couldn't wait to have a baby. I had T.J. when I was twenty, and my son, Brad, at age twenty three. Motherhood was my calling. That may have been partly because my mom always wanted another child, and we often talked about how I would help take care of it. I made her a grandmother when she was barely 40 years old.

My mother was such an attractive woman, so gentle, and I meant everything to her. My dad was jealous of that relationship; but he knew better than to come between us in a serious way, although he certainly tried to. Mama's lack of self esteem, which came from her past and was accelerated by my dad's behavior, caused her to stay with him even after he broke his promises many times, his promises of "I will never do it again."

Yes, motherhood was my job, and I loved it. I loved being "room mother" for my kids, and I loved being "Brownie leader" and "Cub Scout leader." I loved being there when they came home, ready to talk about their day. I not only loved my kids, but I liked them as well. Those were the days when many of us women stayed home, took care of the kids while our husbands worked. I was very determined to be a stay at home mom because my mother worked outside the home at a time when most women did not.

I hated being a latch key kid; I hated coming home to an empty house, especially when my friends' moms were all at home. I loved it when there were holidays and my mom was home, baking cookies, etc. That was fun. The weird part about my mom working in the fifties was that she didn't want to work; she wanted to stay home with me. However, my dad made her work. He said, "You're not going to sit around the house all day while I have to work." This was a different side of the stereotypical abusive man who wanted control of his wife. I think part of his attitude centered around not wanting my mom to get too close to me.

Perhaps he was jealous of her being able to stay at home.

Both of my parents soon became government workers, my mom at the Social Security Administration, and my dad at the U.S. Treasury Agency. I am very proud of how they became self made individuals.

I was lonely and sometimes scared being home alone, but I never complained. On the farm when I was only six, I came home on the school bus alone and was alone in the house for hours before my parents returned from work. I remember rain and thunder storms that were scary, and I remember standing at the kitchen window and looking at the dirt road leading to our farm — hoping to see their car arriving. Yeah, poor me. That was a different era.

In those days, children often had to fit into the plans of the parents. Now, many parents plan their lives around their children. Either extreme may not be the best thing for the child. There were a few months that both of my parents worked a night shift. So rather than leave me at home alone, I had to sleep in the car parked outside the bakery where my mom worked. I remember blankets and pillows so it must have been fall or spring. I could not have been comfortable in a car during the north Texas winters or summers. As I said, that was a different time. Mother came out to check on me from time to time, and I did love those hot glazed donuts. In fact, that was a love affair that lasted most of my life.

Talk about a different era. When my kids went to first grade, I went with them on that first day, which may have not been necessary; but that's what most of us did. On my first day of school, my mom offered to go with me. However, my dad said that would be silly; I could just ride the bus, find my class, and my aunt would be in her class (12th grade) if I needed someone. I went to an old fashioned school in Petrolia, Texas, that housed grades one through 12. Perhaps other kids did have their moms there, because I still remember that no one was with me.

Oh, well, maybe those things made me stronger.

Man, do I feel differently now about women staying home without acquiring job skills in case something happens to that marriage with the white picket fence. I will come back to that later. Of course, with the economy of today, few women plan on staying home for long without returning to work soon after the children are a few years old. Plus, I think everyone should be able to support ones' self. I learned that the hard way and a little late.

Chapter 2

I feel that Dan and I had a good life, a good marriage; but not perfect. I always felt there was something missing, and I would not be surprised to hear that he sometimes felt the same. He once said that we married young, perhaps to escape our families. That comment surprised me, because that certainly wasn't true for me. In fact, I hesitated leaving my mom because I feared what my dad might do to her if I was not there. However, I think he got along better with her after my exit; he had her all to himself.

Dan entered the Computer Science degree program in the fall of 1961, when the field was new and exciting. We lived in Tallahassee for a couple of years, he in graduate school and I attending undergraduate classes. I will always remember how Dan taught me to start our old Chevy on a hill by popping the clutch as the car rolled forward or backward. Thankfully, Tallahassee had a lot of hills. We also had to hang a plastic Clorox bottle filled with sand on our gear shift – to keep if from slipping out of gear. We had little money at that time, and couldn't afford to have the car repaired.

We later moved to Battle Creek, Michigan, where Dan worked for one of the major food companies; there T.J. was born in 1963. Two things stand out in my mind regarding Battle Creek – the first being the smell of cereal in many parts of the city, along with the long procession of trains carrying that cereal to market.

The second memory is not so pleasant. Shortly after T.J. was born, I almost died. I began to scream in pain, and I will always remember the nurse patting me and saying that this was just part of it. Finally, the doctor was summoned (not the doctor who delivered T.J.); I had been bleeding internally, and I had no blood pressure. The doctor told Dan that I might not make it.

However, this specialty doctor saved my life; I was given three pints of blood and I remained in intensive care for three days. By the way, a couple of years later, my gynecologist in New York said after reviewing my records that it appeared to be the fault of the doctor who delivered T.J. He was not a certified gynecologist; his background had been in family practice. Since we were new to the area, I chose him due to a recommendation from one of Dan's coworkers. My New York doctor said my old records stated that my problem came from "a tear in the vault of the vagina." It also stated that the doctor used forceps. Those things happen, but it would have been comforting for me if the doctor had told me what happened, instead of letting me think that it was a big mystery or perhaps a problem with me.

Mother told me later that when Dan called them from Battle Creek to tell them that I might not make it and that I was in intensive care, she almost lost it on the phone. My dad saw her face and became angry at her response; in fact he would not change their prior plans and come on to see me. They came in a couple of weeks as they had originally planned. Daddy still did not want Mother to get too concerned about me. Weird.

Within a couple of years, Dan's company transferred him to their White Plains, New York, office; we found an apartment in Ossining, New York, which was near White Plains, in Westchester County. We drove through the lovely area of Sleepy Hollow many times, and I continued to take college courses in nearby Valhalla. Ossining was the home of the prison, Sing-Sing – as well as the home of "Colombo" actor, Peter Faulk. I mention that because there were signs in the windows of several stores announcing that Faulk was born in Ossining.

We were in New York for the big "Black Out of 1965"- as well as the garbage strike, and the Worlds Fair. I will always remember driving into the city on Sundays to visit the art galleries. I am very grateful for having had the opportunity to live in that area of the country.

We finally made it back to Dallas, Texas, where Brad was born in 1966, and we were near both sets of grandparents. My life was filled with raising the kids, going to college, oil painting, travel with Dan, and becoming certified to teach Montessori School. I decided teaching small children was not my calling; I loved the teaching part, but the "policing" of the kids was not for me. However, I did hang in there and graduated *cum laude* with a Bachelors of General Studies Degree at the University of Texas at Dallas in 1979 – not a degree that was helpful in getting a job. I originally applied at UTD to obtain a degree in Occupational Therapy, but later learned that degree plan had been discontinued. I wonder how different my life would have been had I gotten that degree; I feel sure it would have helped me acquire a job.

Of course, during those years, I did not feel I needed a job. I loved being at home, painting, doing my own thing, being there for my kids even when they were teenagers, spending time with my mom; and money was not an issue. Dan had developed a couple of companies, sold them, and was doing well financially. He was very understanding about our finances, saying that we were equal partners, and that I did my part in raising the kids (great kids, at that). Like most dads back then, Dan had to miss some of the early times with T.J. and Brad while he was getting his career started. He more than made up for that later.

When Dan and I married, I weighed around 125 pounds, had a tiny waist, and people often told me I looked somewhat like Elizabeth Taylor. In fact, I have heard that comparison all my life, no matter what I weighed. Believe me, I know the resemblance is slight. As the years went by, the pounds piled on. I tried almost every diet out there. I once lost 75 pounds at Weight Watchers, but gained it back. I told my daughter that even when I got the weight off, I felt some type of void. I was addicted to sweets, especially chocolate. As a child on the farm, I often came home and mixed up cocoa powder and sugar and ate it! Grannie had taught me that delicacy. I hesitate to blame a slow metabolism, but I think there might be a little truth to that. I knew I ate enough sweets to be 40 or 50 pounds overweight, but I never could understand being 100 pounds overweight.

I tried everything to lose the weight: calorie counting, diet pills, hypnosis, therapy, the supervised medical liquid diets, most of the "buy your food" type programs, the AA type programs, even the injections from the urine of pregnant women. It seems that most diets work as long as you stick with them. Was I hiding something under all that fat? I am sure it wouldn't take a psychological genius to see that my lonely and frightening days as a child probably led me to continue soothing myself with sweets. However, is knowing the cause always a solution to the problem? I don't think so, no matter what the TV therapists say. I will return to this subject later.

In 1977, Dan and I bought a lovely two story home in northeast Dallas. It was on a quiet, tree lined street. To make things even nicer for me, a few years later my mom and her new husband moved just a couple of blocks away. He didn't have a problem with our spending a lot of time together; I picked her up almost every day, and we walked at a local track, ate lunch, etc. I am so grateful for those times.

My dad died in 1981, of a massive coronary at the age of 58. He was a brilliant man, a hard worker, an ethical man - ethical in areas that did not include the treatment of his wife. I never came to terms with how I could love and admire him even though he mistreated my mom so badly. He once yelled at me, "By God, you may not love me, but you damn sure are going to respect me!" As an adult I came to realize that he and I never had a real relationship; I wasn't sure he even loved me. His only relationship was with my mom. Mother once told me that she knew from the beginning that there would be problems between my dad and myself.

She said that when he came back from World War II, I was a beautiful, talkative toddler – the apple of her eye. He had missed those first two years, and was rather jealous of Mother's attention to me. She told me of a time right after he had gotten back home from the war; the three of us were walking outside, about to walk through a gate. I was bare footed and toddling in front of them. He thought I was not walking fast enough, and he lifted his foot and tried to shove me on through the gate. I fell down in stickers and began to cry. Mother said she let him have it, telling him that he had better never mistreat me again. He heeded her words, at least most of the time.

Chapter 3

Now I would like to go to 1989, the year my daughter, T.J., came out as lesbian at age 25. I had figured out her situation even before she told me; it was when she was away on a weekend trip, and I started thinking...I had noticed her voice on the phone with a particular woman. Her voice was different than when I heard her talking to a boy; she was more alive, more vibrant.

That weekend I told Dan that I didn't think we would see T.J. get married. He wondered where all the boys were since she was so attractive and intelligent. I felt I had the answer, but I didn't say anything. After T.J. returned from her trip, she came to my house, and we sat in the living room chatting. I knew her "friend" was about to leave the state for a university teaching position. So I asked T.J. what she was going to do when she left. She responded with, "That's what I want to talk to you about."

Her revelation that she was lesbian was not an unhappy shock to me, partly because I was prepared for it - mainly because she seemed so happy about it. The shock that she was leaving the state with her partner did not hit me at first; that came later. At the time, I had a perfect response, and she sent me flowers the next day. She was not yet ready to tell others, so I had to keep her secret from everyone for a couple of weeks. That was not easy for me, especially when one of my good friends leaned over to me during a movie to tell me a lesbian joke.

It began to dawn on me that T.J. would be leaving, and I became sad about that. Her plans had been to stay in Dallas and, with her dad's help, open up a day care for kids. She had recently graduated with a degree in Psychology, and was about to receive a master's degree in Child Development (She later earned a PhD in Marriage and Family Counseling).

I began to worry about her career with children. Would that now be jeopardized due to her orientation? That would be so unfair, but some people have little knowledge about this issue and have a lot of misinformation. I started worrying about her safety. I began to have questions for T.J., like "Are you sure?" "Couldn't you just be friends like Oprah and Gayle?" (I actually did say that). She just rolled her eyes at me after that comment.

I began to look at myself for blame. Was it because she didn't see me being very affectionate to her dad? Was it because I got her interested in the women's movement when she was too young? I did buy her that "women's equality" necklace that she wore a lot when she was only about 12 years old, and there was that Ms Magazine that came in the mail. Oh, I remembered an incident when she was in junior high.

Her male English teacher (a coach) had assigned the class a writing project: the boys were to write about the family car and the girls were to write about their bedroom! T.J. came home very disappointed because we had just purchased a new van, and she wanted to write about it. I advised her to do as the teacher had asked and write about her bedroom, but to add a note at the end of her paper saying she felt the assignment was sexist, and that she would have really liked to have written about the van. She wrote the note.

You know, a year or so later a student who had that teacher said he mentioned that T.J. Stone was the only student he had taught that thought for herself. That's nice, but did I push the women's equality thing too much and too early? No, there are feminists who are not lesbians, and probably some lesbians who are not feminists.

It may sound strange that, I, a stay at home mom, was so into the women's movement. However, I saw their message as offering a choice to women.

I learned from my dad that if you don't understand something, get a book and learn about it. So I went to a mainstream book store and found the book called *Now That You Know: What Every Parent Should Know about Homosexuality*. I read the stories of many parents who had faced this issue, and I realized what I already knew in my heart – that T.J.'s orientation was as natural to her as having blue eyes and curly hair.

Some parents mourn the dreams they had for their gay children. I didn't have a problem there, because I never got caught up in seeing T.J. walk down that isle in marriage. I wasn't against it; I just felt that she might be giving up some of her independence with marriage. Grandchildren would be nice, but not a requirement for me to have a fulfilling life. However, she assured me that she did want to have a child. By the way, that child is now a 14 years old boy, born via donor insemination.

When Dan learned that T.J. was gay, his reaction to her news was that of understanding, but a real dread concerning her move from Dallas. At first he didn't know how all of this would play out, but he knew for sure he wasn't going to lose a daughter over this new information. As he said to me, "Things don't always turn out the way we think they will."

Her brother, Brad, guessed her situation without realizing it. I remember standing in my kitchen, telling him that T.J., as well as her friend, would be moving out of state, and that she would be working on a PhD. He immediately said, "What's going on, some kind of a lesbian thing?" He could tell by the look on my face that that was the case. I suppose he knew that it would take something very important to cause her to leave Dallas. T.J. had planned on telling him, but it just came out. Brad did not have a problem with this new revelation because he had always been accepting of that issue. In fact, he often corrected his friends if they made anti-gay remarks.

I will always remember when T.J. and her partner came to our house as a couple for the first time. I hate to say it, but it was really strange for me to see them reach out to casually touch one another or briefly hold hands. It was new to me; I was not offended, just surprised. I began to realize how careful they had to be concerning any show of affection in public. How unfair, but that was twenty years ago – not that it's changed that much in parts of the South.

I also remember T.J. telling me by phone (after they moved away) about purchasing a bed, and how careful they had to be when picking it out and especially when it was delivered. They didn't want to risk possible problems by letting the delivery guys know that they were a couple. Safety is always a concern. A rather melancholy thing that sticks out in my mind concerning those early days was when I visited T.J. and her partner for the first time; it must have been October of 1989. It's something that I have never mentioned to anyone because it's a small thing and my feelings about it are hard to explain. As I walked up to their lovely home, I saw lit jack-o-lanterns in their windows, facing out to the world. Tears briefly came to my eyes. To me, the scene said, "Hey, we are like everyone else. We are a family, and we are celebrating the holiday. Don't be unkind to us." That's what I wanted for her, for people to accept her for her inner goodness and to be kind to her.

Dan and I continued to go through the stages of total acceptance of our lesbian daughter; it was a quick process. We too had to "come out" about her orientation to our friends and family. With a few exceptions, that went very smoothly. Our closest friends thought highly of T.J. and that did not change. I remember one friend (outside our main circle) commented with, "What a waste. She is so beautiful."

A close family member was not accepting at all, letting her religion speak instead of her heart. She no longer mentioned T.J.'s name to me or asked about her ever again. My mom did not understand T.J.'s situation so she called a Methodist minister (not *her* Methodist minister) and talked it out. She wrestled with the religious angle, but decided it wasn't her place to judge. She became very supportive of T.J., and she and her husband visited her right away (which meant a long drive for them). I hesitate to mention where T.J. lives, always guarded concerning a possible safety issue. It's in the South.

In the February 28, 1990, issue of the *Dallas Morning News*, I saw a "Dear Abby" column, entitled "Group Helps Parents of Homosexuals." Abby advised a distressed mom to contact the group called Parents and Friends of Lesbians and Gays (It later changed its name to Parents, Families, and Friends of Lesbians and Gays, PFLAG). I kept the article for almost a year; then in 1991, I called the National Office to inquire about a local chapter. I thought I might be able to help other parents. However, I learned that there was not a chapter in Dallas, even though the organization began in New York in 1972. There was a lesbian couple in our area that acted as contacts for parents. Long story short: I contacted them, learned of a few other interested parents, and a handful of us founded the PFLAG/Dallas chapter in 1992.

I began my work with PFLAG as Vice President of the local chapter; but within nine months I became it's President, and I also handled the Helpline. The chapter grew from just a few members to often having a 100 people at our meetings, and many more receiving our newsletter. As I always announced at our meeting, we worked through "support, education, and advocacy." I worked hard to balance those three, because when new parents came through our door, they often were not ready for an advocacy role. However, they certainly needed support and were eager to learn more about the gay issue so that they could correct the misinformation out there.

Some of our parents were ready to march in the gay pride parade right away, but we never pushed them to do so. Once parents marched in the parade, they were forever changed. The crowd of gays and lesbians cheering us and shouting "thanks" was such an over powering emotion for us. We represented the parents they wished they had.

Our meetings usually consisted of short announcements, a speaker, and then we divided up into "rap groups," which was the heart of PFLAG. There they could share their thoughts and concerns relating to their gay loved one. Other parents who had gone through similar experiences were very helpful. We also welcomed gay and lesbians to join in the rap groups. We felt it was important for the parents to make contact with other gay people in addition to their child. The parents helped the gays and lesbians and vice versa.

Our speakers ranged from therapists to ministers, from respected gay and lesbian leaders to Dallas community leaders. My greatest achievement regarding speakers was getting Mayor Ron Kirk to speak to us in 1996 (239 people came to hear him). I worked long and hard to get him, calling his office many times, speaking to several of his assistants. I received the greatest compliment from him as he began to speak that night.

As the applause was dying down, he said to the audience, "You had better applaud Pat Stone. She's one of the most tenacious people I have ever met. She got hold of me and wouldn't let go!" By the way, he gave such a supportive and enthusiastic presentation, telling us about his gay cousin who had AIDS and how Ron Kirk's mom took him in. You may have seen Mr. Kirk on CNN during the summer of 2008 as a vocal Obama supporter. He was later appointed to Obama's cabinet as his trade representative. I have always admired Ron Kirk, and Dallas was lucky to have had him as mayor. Things were getting better in Dallas by that time regarding the gay issue, and I think PFLAG played its part in creating that change.

However, when we first started out in 1992, it was rather scary. At first, no one wanted to use their phone number for the chapter, fearing reprisals. I volunteered my home number for the helpline. We had a few minor threats, but nothing too serious. I enjoyed doing the helpline; it was a way of keeping in contact with the pain that parents were going through, and the misinformation that was out there.

I got calls from parents from all walks of life, from all religions. Those that seemed to have the hardest time were the parents from the more fundamental religions. Many times they put away their religious views in order to support their child; others chose their religion over their child. I sometimes got calls from gay kids who had been thrown out of their homes; young boys crying, saying they didn't want to be gay. And some people say to be gay is a choice? Perhaps it is for a few people (mainly a few women); however, from my experience, most gays and lesbians tell me it was not a choice for them.

In PFLAG I found my "voice," my purpose in life. I had never been a public speaker, but when my child's well being was on the line, I was ready to try to make some changes in attitudes regarding the gay issue. Several of us parents spoke at school boards, at city council meetings, at corporations, on TV, on the radio, anywhere we thought we could make a difference. At first, PFLAG was "my thing." Later Dan became very much involved with me. He even led one of the rap groups at our meetings, and sometimes joined me in speaking engagements. He had never been a "joiner," but PFLAG was different for him. He saw it as a civil rights issue, and he wanted to do his part. At first it was all about our daughter, but it soon became a much bigger issue than that for us. It was the right thing to do, and it affected so many people, so many families.

On August 21, 1992, we had been a chapter for only seven months. Four of us Moms (Sandy, Shirley, Kathy, and myself) decided to picket the National Affairs Briefing Meeting at the Dallas Convention Center. Many of the noted conservative politicians were attending, including the first President Bush; they had just come from the Republican Convention in Houston, TX, where unkind things were said about gays and lesbians. President Bush allowed the Christian Right to demonstrate its powers and influence within the party by speaking at the convention. People like Robertson, Falwell, and Buchanan criticized Clinton for being "pro homosexual."

We had to make certain we were not protesting a particular party due to our 501(c)(3) status; we were protesting the disparaging remarks made against our kids, remarks that we felt put them in jeopardy. My sign said "We love our gay and lesbian children." (I carried that sign to 14 events.) We were joined in our protest by various gay and lesbian groups, even the Cathedral of Hope (the largest predominately gay and lesbian church in the world which resided in Dallas). Dan came with us moms in case there was trouble.

The opposition was in force; and as we walked by, they waved their Bibles and yelled unkind things to us. After a candlelight vigil, police on horseback arrived and got in front of everyone, making sure the crowd did not get too close to the doors. A few protesters were arrested; It was a scary, but empowering evening. When I returned home, there was a message on my answering machine. It was our son, Brad; he had disguised his voice, sounding very professional. He said in his very deep tone of voice, "Uh, this is agent Peterson from the FBI. I understand you have been protesting the President of the United States. Please get your things in order." Brad has always made me smile.

As I mentioned before, I made it clear to our PFLAGers that it was not expected that they all get involved in protests, parades, or speeches. Advocacy was not for everyone, and it could be achieved in smaller ways like telling their family and friends about their gay loved one. Putting a face to this issue has always been so important. Writing letters to their senators and congressmen was an additional way to be an advocate. I wrote Barbara Bush soon after starting our chapter on January 30, 1992, telling her about my daughter and PFLAG, and asking her to help us in any way possible, whether in public or private. I received this letter from her on March 4, 1992, on White House stationery:

"I so much appreciated your heartfelt letter telling me about your daughter and your deep concern for her future. As a mother and a grandmother, I too worry about the future of our children and our nation. I am very much aware of the organization PFLAG, and have been touched by the many kind letters I have received from members and supporters expressing similar concerns. I firmly believe that we cannot tolerate discrimination against any individuals or groups in our country. Such treatment always brings with it pain and perpetuates hate and intolerance. I appreciate so much your encouraging me to help change attitudes. Your words speak eloquently of your love for your daughter and your compassion for all gay Americans and their families." With all best wishes, Warmly, (signed) Barbara Bush.

Between the years of 1993 to 1995, there were many opportunities for me to speak at various events, and I would like to share a few with you:

I spoke at the joint hearing before the Commissioner of Education and the 1993 State Textbook Subject Area Committee in Austin, Texas. Since Texas was responsible for many of the textbooks across the country, this was an important meeting. Our opposition included the women from the Texas Eagle Forum, who opposed any supportive comments regarding the AIDS situation being mentioned in the health textbooks. One of those women even objected to having the drawing included in the boy's health textbook that showed how to do a self examination of the breast. One of the men on the committee said, "Madam, do you realize that some men also get breast cancer?"

One of the more sad speaking engagements was the Tyler, Texas, Rally (January 8, 1994) in response to the murder of Nick West, who was killed because he was gay. There were many gay and lesbian speakers present that afternoon. I spoke as a parent and member of PFLAG. We wanted to honor Nick West, and we hoped to make a difference in East Texas regarding attitudes of some citizens concerning gays and lesbians.

A very important opportunity was speaking at the Dallas Independent School District Summer Seminar. It was held at the Infomart on July 28, 1994. I spoke concerning gay youth, and it was geared to the school counselors, psychologists, and nurses.

I was also proud to be able to speak at Northern Telcom on "Homophobia in the Workplace on May 16, 1995 – as well as speaking to the Dallas Police Recruit Training class on October 30, 1995. When we spoke to that class, we often were not "speaking to the choir;" but what a great opportunity to make a difference.

I appeared on several local TV shows regarding the gay issue, but the most prominent one (most viewers) was the Project 8 Family First town meeting in Plano, Texas. Comments were aired on the nightly news on January 11, 1993. There was opposition present at that town meeting; but it was a great opportunity to be part of the dialogue.

As you can see, there was a big change in attitudes regarding the gay issue between 1992, when we started our local PFLAG chapter in Dallas to 1996, when Mayor Ron Kirk came to speak to our meeting. In fact, on July 15, 1996, there was a huge article in the *Dallas Morning News* about my family and other PFLAG members, entitled "When the closet door opens." It even included a large color photo of my entire family – Dan, myself, T.J., Brad, my Mom (Martha), and my grandson. It was a very complementary article written by Ellen Sweets.

In addition to that article, on October 18, 1995, in celebration of National Coming Out Day, there was "A Family Outing" at the State Fair of Texas. A photo of my daughter and her family was on the brochures for the event. That photo was also on the back of some of the Dallas city buses advertising the celebration. We met and chatted with Chastity Bono the day of the event; she was one of the speakers, as well as Candace Gingrich. National Coming Out Day was a way of celebrating being out, but the advise to gays and lesbians was to take their time with it, that it was a process, involving many steps. In connection with "A Family Outing at the State Fair of Texas," T.J. and I were interviewed by our local Channel 8, ABC station; it aired during our nightly news on October 8, 1995.

Yes, looking back at those events and articles, it was obvious that we had come a long way. Of course there was work remaining to be done and there still is, but what strides have been made both locally and nationally. PFLAG is still out there supporting families and helping to change attitudes. I see from their web site that there are now over 500 chapters nation wide and over 200,000 members and supporters. What a great organization; I feel honored to have been part of it. I am a life time member, and my email address is still pflagpat@aol.com.

On May 6, 1995, the local Dallas Federal Club (affiliated with HRC, the Human Rights Campaign) asked my family to speak at one of their wonderful luncheons. T.J. was unable to fly in for it, and Brad already had out of town plans. So I asked my mom to attend, never dreaming that she would do it. She had always been so shy and was certainly not a public speaker. You should have seen her sitting on that stage with Dan and me. She seemed perfectly at home, and was very comfortable speaking about her granddaughter's journey. In fact, on one occasion, she took the microphone back from me, saying she had something else to add. The audience loved her.

I should have known that she would rise to the occasion. As a child I associated weakness with my mom; however, as I got older I saw how she always showed great strength in a crisis, especially when it involved helping other people. I have always felt such love for her and very protective of her. My friends and my kids' friends also loved her, often referring to her as "Mema."

An additional gay and lesbian event that Dan and I attended was the 1995 Dallas Black Tie Dinner (the largest one in the nation). Former Texas Governor, Ann Richards, was the key note speaker. You may remember her speech at the 1988 Democratic National Convention in Atlanta when she said, "Poor George (Bush). He can't help it. He was born with a silver foot in his mouth."

The Black Tie Dinner is a non profit organization that raises funds for gay, lesbian, bisexual, and transgendered groups and their supporters in North Texas (including PFLAG/Dallas). The night Ms Richards spoke was such a fun evening; she had the place rolling with laughter. We had several PFLAG tables there filled with our parents, and we marveled at the elegance of the event. Also, from a personal point of view, I have a lovely picture of Ann Richards and myself; in fact, I often used it as my "before" photo, before I lost 100 pounds! That had to be the heaviest I had ever been, a whopping 265 pounds!

That leads me to the miracle pills that helped me lose that 100 pounds, "Phen-Fen." Before I started that medication, I was down to my lowest point emotionally concerning my weight. I felt a real hopelessness. I found notes that I had made during that time, and it was obvious I had been very depressed. I mentioned that I only enjoyed four things in my life: playing with my dog, Sandy, going to Las Vegas with Dan and my friends, leading the PFLAG meetings, and laughing with my son, Brad.

I said that I was not suicidal, but I knew how I would do it if I was – in the closed garage with the car running. One of my quotes from my notes was: "I think it might be easier to be "up" about life when you feel sure your time here is limited rather than not knowing if you will live one hour or 20 more years…I am sure when I start losing weight, the depression will lift and the world will look better."

Luckily (or not), I soon saw an article in the paper about "Phen-Fen," and I immediately checked it out, and began the program. It truly did seem like a miracle - no more hunger, no more cravings. I wrote down the calories and fat count of everything I ate, but there were times I didn't care if I ate at all. The pounds began to melt away. I was one of the lucky ones that took the drugs over a year with no obvious side effects or medical harm. I had lost 60 of the 100 pounds when my life took a shocking turn.

Chapter 4

I now need to introduce my good friend, John Selig, to you. I feel comfortable using his full name since he is very "out" and has appeared on numerous TV shows, on radio, and in many articles. You most likely have noticed that I do not use the last names of most people due to honoring their privacy.

I met John when he was doing a lot of photography in the gay community, and he became a regular at our PFLAG meetings; he was also quite the activist. He was a close friend of both Dan and myself. He had been married for years and had a son. Well, John gave me a suggestion for a speaker for our July, 11, 1996, PFLAG meeting; she was a well known lesbian activist named Lory Masters. I remember his saying, "You will love Lory."

I emailed Lory, and she agreed to speak; she said she greatly admired PFLAG and the work I had done. I requested her biography, and was it impressive! She owned Master Realtors, and she had been a pioneer for human rights from the age of twenty and had helped create and/or founded such organizations as The Oasis Drug and Alcohol Program, The Women's Chorus of Dallas, The Extra Mile Awards and The Women's Motorcycle Club of Dallas.

She had served the local, state and national community as an emcee, fundraiser, facilitator, and speaker. She was currently the National Chair of a Capital Campaign (40 Million) for the Cathedral of Hope; National Human Rights Campaign Board Emeritus; National Board Emeritus

Member of An Uncommon "Legacy" Foundation and a National Advisory Board Member of the National Center for Lesbian Rights. Major awards received had included: "Saint's Alive" by the Cathedral of Hope, Voted "Best Realtor" four out of six years, 1992 Schwab Award by the Texas Human Rights Foundation, 1992 "Humanitarian of the Year" (Kuchling Award) by the Human Rights Campaign Black Tie Dinner, 1989 "Grand Marshall" of the Dallas Pride Parade, 1988 winner of The Extra Mile Award.

She was profiled in Out Magazine in 1994, as well as appearing in 50-50 Magazine in 1995. (Years later she was featured in Women's Magazine in 1998, and Lory was listed in the top 10 Most Powerful Lesbians in the USA in Girlfriend magazine in 2001.) These were only a few of her many accomplishments.

Her persona that night included such an interesting combination of factors. She was a blonde, attractive, activist to be admired and respected due to her many accomplishments in the gay and lesbian community. Her presentation was never boring as she related some of these achievements to us. She came off as very humorous as she shared some of her early experiences of coming out. She had an appealing touch of bawdiness perhaps due to her slightly raspy voice. Then there was the vulnerability when she talked about her mom and her daughter, and the hope that things would continue to get better for her community.

Her strength was overwhelming as she told us how things used to be, how the gay bars were routinely raided by the police when she was in her twenties, how her daughter was sometimes teased at school because her mom was gay. She said that when people of her age were younger, "we were told that we were very bad people. We knew better."

Lory painted a fun picture of her motorcycle days, and she spoke with pride of her many years of sobriety (25 years on Nov. 8, 2008). She was a strong, independent, "bigger than life" woman. She was approaching fifty years old so she had seen a lot in those 30 years, including many positive changes. She praised PFLAG for it's contribution to those changes, on the local, national, and international level.

Lory talked about the importance of the coming out process. She said, "If every lesbian and gay man stood up for just one day, there would be no more discrimination because people would see us for who we are and what we are. We are a very diverse group. We are loving, caring, Christian, wonderful people." She also encouraged the PFLAG parents to continue to come out to their families and friends regarding having a gay or lesbian child. She said, "Let the world know it's OK with you. Let others know that you want equal rights for your child, not special rights." Lory advised the parents to "be kind to your children; things you say can cut very deep."

Our audience loved her presentation; she was a big hit. As Lory left that night, she gave me a big hug and said, "Let's do lunch sometime." I agreed, but figured it would never happen. I assumed it was just something she said to be nice (which it was), and what connection would we have to warrant a lunch meeting?

Several of our PFLAG members were away on vacation the night Lory spoke; so as I often did with other speakers, I taped her presentation. At home I started making several copies of her speech, listening as I went about my daily tasks. What happened next was a total surprise to me, and led me along a complex journey of self discovery. However, it also led to family turmoil and a reevaluation of my new found voice, my purpose.

From what seemed to me to be out of the blue, two weeks after she spoke at PFLAG, these romantic, sexual feelings came to me regarding Lory. Was it hearing her voice and her message on the tape over and over? I did remember showing her photo to my friends and talking about her presentation, speaking of how unique she was.

What was all this about? Was it a crush on this particular woman, or did it indicate something about my orientation? I didn't really know Lory very well so it had to be a crush, right? But a crush on a woman?

I had never had those feelings before for a woman (or a man). The more I thought about it, the more I began to wonder if by seeing her, I was seeing part of myself. She was an activist (not that I could compare with her accomplishments); she was close to my age; she dressed similarly to myself (rather feminine). But then, perhaps she also had qualities that I would have liked to have had; she was openly sensual; she was very out going; she had an attitude.

I continued to wrestle with the meaning of all of this. Was I lesbian? If so, why had I not seen it sooner? On the one hand, I marveled at this new insight; I was happy to have finally had those special feelings. It was the missing piece of the puzzle. I had thought I would live my entire life without those feelings. On the other hand, what would this mean to my family situation, after being married for 35 years? Would Dan understand that this was not a reflection on him? What would it mean regarding PFLAG and the Dallas gay and lesbian community?

Chapter 5

I will now chronicle most of the events and discoveries that took place during those two important years (important for me) of 1996 -1997. I have kept numerous notes, emails, letters, faxes, and articles regarding this sensitive time.

I felt I had to talk to someone about this new predicament. So I called my friend, John Selig, and told him that I would like to come by and run something by him. He said that would be great, and he asked when would I like to come. I said I was on my way; it was Sunday afternoon, August 4, 1996. He later told me that he wondered what in the world was going on. He was more than a little surprised when I told him about my feelings for Lory. He was not encouraging.

He thought a lot of Dan and loved us as a couple as well as individuals. He didn't want me to make any quick decisions that I might later regret. I will always remember his comment, "Hell, I'm a gay man, and I love Lory Masters!" So in other words, be sure about my feelings and what they meant. However, on the other hand, he was very supportive of me and my dilemma; I think he felt a little responsible since he had encouraged me to get Lory as a speaker. There was no fault here – by anyone. John advised me to get counseling to help me handle the situation. I resisted doing that.

Dan and I already had a trip planned to visit T.J in August. So on Monday, August 26, 1996, I confided in her about what I had been going through. She, her partner and I went out to lunch. By the way, the reason I never mention the name of T.J.'s partner is that they broke up after being together 12 years, and I want to honor her privacy. T.J. is now very happy with her current partner, who she has been with since 2000.

Back to the lunch and my confession. T.J. and I have always been close, and she knew a lot about my various struggles. I said to her, "I have had special feelings for someone; who do you think it is?" I told her that she had heard the name. (I had sent her the tape of Lory speaking; that was before I began having feelings for her. I should have known then that something was brewing.) T.J. mentioned a PFLAG dad, never dreaming it would be for a woman.

What an insensitive way for me to tell her about this new situation. Man, they say when an older person comes out, they become a teenager again! T.J. was very surprised about the lesbian angle. However, she said that she feared that someday down the line that she would get a call saying I was in clinical depression. Guess she saw something that outsiders did not. On the outside, Dan and I appeared to be the perfect PFLAG couple. T.J. was very supportive of me, but she (like John Selig) encouraged me to get counseling. I continued to resist that suggestion. She was caught in the middle of this, trying to support me, but also being concerned about her dad. She advised me to take this slowly, but to follow my heart.

The last night of our trip, we all watched a fabulous movie, called *Losing Chase*; Chase was the name of one of the female characters. It starred Helen Mirren, Kyra Sedgwick and Beau Bridges, directed by Kevin Bacon. I believe it was on HBO. It involved a married woman who later realized she was lesbian. It was a rather uneasy experience watching it, since all but Dan knew about my situation. I was hoping he would be impressed with the movie, and that it would be meaningful and helpful when I told him my news.

After returning to Dallas from my visit with T.J., I felt better having told a family member about what I had been going through. She tried very hard to remain neutral, but supportive. I knew I had put her in a very awkward position, but I also knew I needed her help. However, telling another person made the situation seem more real and rather scary.

I returned to my busy schedule of meetings in the gay community and my PFLAG work. I was on the board of a youth hot line, and it was also time to be planning for the Gay Pride Parade as well as the Black Tie Dinner event. I was booking two upcoming speakers for PFLAG – Louise Young for September and Victor Moralis for August.

Louise was (and is) a well know lesbian activist; in fact, she and her partner, Vivienne Armstrong, rode in President Clinton's first inaugural parade on the float, "The Family of America," representing gay and lesbian Americans. I became friends with them and admired them very much. (They are a very respected couple who have been together for over 30 years, and they were married in California in 2008.)

Victor Moralis was running for U.S. Senator at that time. However, I told him he could not talk about the race, but to just dwell on his beliefs and positions. On September 6th, I met Hillary Clinton at a fundraiser at the Fairmont Hotel. I thanked her for all she and her husband had done for equal rights for gays and lesbians, which included my daughter.

Of course, no matter how busy I was, I continued to be engulfed with the new feelings, the new awareness. What to do next? Don't ask me why, but I felt the next step was to tell Lory. I certainly didn't expect anything from her; she only knew me as President of PFLAG. Why dump this on her? I can only tell you that I felt it was important that I talk to her about it. It was an overpowering need. I guess my brain told me that nothing would come of it, but my teenaged heart wanted to risk it. There's no logic to this. I certainly was not going to approach her with the hope of any type of relationship at that time. I was married and had not even discussed these puzzling feelings with my husband. I began the unbelievable task of trying to schedule a lunch date with her.

My excuse was that I wanted to meet with her to get her input on ideas of how to further reach out to the gay community regarding PFLAG. After all, she had even suggested that we have lunch. Yeah, right. So I began the calls to her office. She told me that she would love to do lunch, and she scheduled me for a particular time. Well, to make a painful, long story short, she cancelled me five times! She had a very busy schedule, and something was always coming up – an unexpected closing on a house, an unplanned trip, etc. That was a big red flag for me; I knew then that I would not want a relationship with someone who was that busy. Of course, I wasn't looking for a relationship; not sure what I was looking for...

Finally, a date was set for Tuesday, September 10, 1996, at 11 am. I met Lory at a Chinese restaurant for lunch. I had lost another 10 pounds by then, making it a 70 pound loss; I guess I thought I was looking pretty cute. I think one of the first things she said after we sat down was, "I've got to smoke" as she grabbed her lighter. That was not even a turn off for me, although I have tried to get her to stop smoking several times. We began talking about PFLAG, about weight issues, etc. She said the way she lost weight was due to a divorce about four years ago, from a woman named, Evie; they had been together seven years. I told her I had been married for 35 years, and she said, "to the same man?" I said yes, but she couldn't believe it.

We did talk a little about PFLAG and my role in the organization. As our small talk dwindled, I told her that there was something else I felt I needed to tell her. I explained that about two weeks after she had spoken to PFLAG, these mysterious, romantic feelings came to me about her. I didn't know if it had something to do with the tape of her speech that I had listened to while making copies. I didn't know what to make of it. I certainly didn't expect anything in return from her, but I just felt the need to tell her. I am sure she was stunned, but she remained calm. More than likely, this was not the first time someone had brought this type of news to her.

She told me that she was flattered, but that she was starting a new relationship at the time. She was very diplomatic and kind to me; she handled this with a lot of class. I explained that I had never had feelings like this for a woman, not anyone really. I told her that I found her to be a very dynamic and strong woman, and I admired her very much. She told me how she also admired all my work at PFLAG and the work I had done in the gay community. She added that it was very important that I get counseling, and gave me the name of someone she would recommend. She remembered other friends who had come out in a similar situation, and how traumatic it had been for them.

I didn't shed any tears, at least not at that time. We continued talking, keeping things as light as possible. However, she make it clear that she wanted to help me through this, that she would be checking on me, and for me to call her anytime. She laughed and said that she wanted a copy of that tape to see what I found so appealing. I found out later that when she returned to her office, she told her secretary that the President of PFLAG might be in love with her! That scared her because she felt some (unfounded) responsibility, and she feared repercussions from Dan, from PFLAG, and from the gay community. I feared all of those things as well, but Lory had no reason to be concerned. She had done nothing but speak at a PFLAG meeting.

As I mentioned earlier, I have kept a lot of information that speaks of the journey of my coming out. Most of it includes communications to T.J. and Lory. As I told both of them, those exchanges became great tools of therapy for me. I also kept notes of my therapy sessions. Taking notes on important events in my life was not a new thing for me. That's just the way I handle things. I still have notes on my poodle, Buffy who died years ago, on the death of my dad, on the 9-11 tragedy, a diary of when my kids were younger, including comments on the Vietnam War.

After talking to Lory, I felt both better and worse. A few people have asked me if I would have acted on my new awareness right away with Lory - if she would have gone along with it. The answer is "no." That was certainly not why I went to her with my news. Dan would have *never* forgiven me if I had done that – plus it would not have been the right thing to do. From a more shallow point of view, I was still overweight at that time; months later after losing the remaining weight, I was left with a 9 pound apron of skin which required a tummy tuck in December. I certainly was not ready to have an intimate encounter with anyone at that time.

Someone also suggested that I was cheating on my husband just by going to Lory before I told Dan of my new feelings. I don't agree, because at that time, I wasn't sure what those feelings were or what they meant. It took time and therapy to fully understand what was going on with me. I wasn't ready to upset Dan before I fully understand the situation. He never chastised me for talking to Lory first.

I didn't regret going to her although I felt badly about putting her in an uncomfortable position. I was disappointed that she was starting a relationship; however, I felt that was not the real reason she was not interested in me, but maybe someday...Man, we do delude ourselves, don't we? I still felt fairly confident that my orientation was lesbian, and that I needed to continue the process of becoming my true self.

The next day, Wednesday, September 11, 1996, I changed my view. I told this to T.J. in a fax. I also wrote Lory a similar letter. I told T.J. that I would no longer burden her, Lory or John Selig with all of this. I was tired of talking about this, and I figured they would soon be tired of listening. I felt trapped by all sides, and I felt the whole thing was rather hopeless, mainly due to my connection to PFLAG. I mentioned that the night before was very hard for me, because the reality had set in that this was an impossible situation due to my position in the gay community and in the PFLAG community.

I told her that I had shed the first tears regarding all of this. I knew my position as a straight parental advocate was powerful, and I hated to lose it. I told T.J. that I decided that I should forget about myself and think of the gay and PFLAG community, that I had lived 53 years without romance, and I could do it a little longer. I thought about my important contacts in the Dallas community – Mayor Ron Kirk, Steve Blow (writer for the *Dallas Morning News*), important contacts at the Dallas Independent School District, etc. I felt that I was one of the last people that the Dallas gay community would want to come out as lesbian. Also, I doubted that a parent coming in our door at PFLAG for the first time, trying to come to terms with having a gay child, would want to face a lesbian President. Not fair, but a reality. This thing was dragging me down.

After getting my fax, T.J. called me late that night. She must have seen some red flags so she decided she needed to intervene, and I'm glad she did. Up until then, she had just been a sounding board for me. I feel I would have come out of this low period soon anyway, because I am too much of a fighter to feel so hopeless and trapped for long. But who knows...She helped turn me around.

T.J. said that the roller coaster ride of emotions were normal, that she remembered them well when she came out seven years ago. She suggested that I continue going to some gay and lesbian functions by myself; I could represent PFLAG as well as myself. She reminded me that I could still be very involved in PFLAG and be lesbian also, and as far as all the valuable contacts I had made, these could be passed on to other PFLAG parents.

She said to quit worrying about what may or may not happen down the line; to stop worrying about disappointing the gay community and the PFLAG community, to think of myself for a change. I had always done for others; now it was time to do what's best for me. She told me to call that therapist that Lory had suggested, and to really look at the many things going on in my life – the orientation issue, the large weight loss, my best friend struggling with ovarian cancer, etc.

One of the most interesting things T.J. said was that it's common to put stumbling blocks in the road (which it seemed I was doing) to show that this can't work. Also, I think she was concerned that I mentioned crying, and she knew I didn't cry easily. (My dad thought that was a sign of weakness.) I knew the crying stage would not last long, mainly because it made my eyes so swollen that I looked terrible. T.J. cautioned me that by my deciding to no longer talk about this situation, I might take it inside and internalize it, causing a deep depression to arise. So I decided to emerge from the "poor, pitiful Pearl" stage. I wrote Lory and told her to not worry about me, that I was pulling myself together and would go to therapy.

I called the therapist the next day. I feel I should not use even her real first name, because therapists like to maintain privacy concerning their clients and their issues. I will refer to her as "Brenda." She had a very calm and pleasant voice over the phone. She asked me basically what was going on with me; and after I gave her a brief run down, she said she could work me in the next day!

Chapter 6

My first therapy appointment was Friday, September 13, 1996. Over the course of the next few months, we talked about many things: my childhood, my weight issues, and, of course, this new realization. I knew that one of the important issues for me was to decide if this was a true orientation discovery or was it a just a crush on this particular woman. However, I also knew that many lesbians have made early statements that they thought at first the attraction was just for a particular woman, not that they were necessarily gay. Most soon realized that they were lesbian. I felt that an additional factor to be gained from therapy was to be able to handle the coming out stages if indeed I decided this was a true orientation issue. I knew it was important for me to separate Lory from the actual orientation question. That was hard for me.

One of the first statements from Brenda was for me to always remember to keep the same basic values I already had. I suppose that meant to not try to change too many things about myself; to stay true to my inner self. She also said that people come out for one of two reasons: They have a relationship and want that person to be honored and acknowledged or the person wants to be who he/she really is. It seemed that I came under the second category.

After extensive discussions with Brenda concerning my childhood, she saw part of the reason I was attracted to Lory. I mentioned in therapy how I loved my mother very much, but I felt she was weak; she was extremely afraid of so many things from spiders to storms. She also took my dad's abuse, never leaving him or getting me out of that situation. I grew up seeing women as having less than strong personalities, and there were not many strong female role models out there in those days.

So when I saw Lory, I saw strength as well as an attractive, vivacious woman. I tried to be sensible and see Lory as a catalyst for my coming out; it was unfortunate that I put so many feelings on her. She once told me that few women ever end up with the first woman they were attracted to. Yes, she dropped several hints, but she was too kind to make it crystal clear to me. I am sure she felt I was too fragile at first to face the fact that we would never have any type of relationship except friendship. As I said before, I always knew our personalities were not suited for an actual relationship, but I still had that attraction to her. Poor Lory, I don't know how she had the patience to put up with me. However, she hung in there, always checking on me.

Brenda pointed out that on July 11th when Lory spoke to PFLAG, I saw the perfect combination of my dad and my mother – the strength and independence of my dad, but the vulnerability of my mom. Plus she had the other thing I needed and still need; she was very demonstrative – she showed affection openly. I soon learned after talking with Lory that her childhood was as challenging as mine, perhaps more so. I seemed to tune in to the little girl she once was; I felt so sorry that she had had been mistreated. It was not a stretch to see, as Brenda pointed out, that it was easier and safer to sympathize with Lory as a child than with my own childhood. Plus, I really cared about Lory, and wanted to know more about her.

Brenda sometimes played "devil's advocate," forcing me to decide for myself what was going on with me. She once told me, "You seem so sure you are gay, but you haven't seriously considered you might not be, have you?" After that session, I was furious with her and with the whole situation. I stormed home, opened my door, looked around my den, and thought, "OK, I can just sit right here and rock along and not deal with this. No one seems to want me to be gay anyway!" I felt like my feelings were not really being considered and taken seriously. I felt like canceling the next appointment with Brenda as well as with the divorce attorney. (She had advised me to see a lawyer before telling Dan.) No, I decided I would cancel her and keep the appointment with the lawyer.

After calming down and thinking things over, I called Brenda's office and left her a message saying, "Just because I haven't questioned if I was really lesbian in your office did not mean I have not done so at home. I do not look at it as a great club that I can not wait to join. Surely you know what I will be giving up if I identify as lesbian. What does it mean when a woman has a strong attraction to a woman and has no attraction to men? Sounds pretty close to being lesbian to me!" I felt better after that rant.

I did not cancel my next appointment with Brenda, and we discussed her maneuver to get me to really think strongly about my position. I admitted that it caused me to see things very clearly, that I was sure this was an orientation issue (separate from my feelings for Lory), and I was ready to proceed with the process. She said that was what was supposed to happen; it reinforced my position and my awareness became stronger and more crystallized. A few sessions later, Brenda said, "You know, you have had those feelings all along; you just have not been aware of them or dealt with them." Then she told me how she defines "denial;" it wasn't what I thought. As she pointed to the air vent on the ceiling, she said, "That vent has been making noise all along; you just have not noticed it until it was pointed out to you." "That's denial," she said.

She also said that I needed to get in touch with my feelings; that could be why I did not see my orientation until later in life. Perhaps others like Lory, who realized they were gay early on, were more in touch with their feelings. As you have already heard, I was raised by a very strict father who frowned on expressions of affection. I remember his making fun of aunts who came to visit saying, "Just watch, they can't wait to start hugging everyone." I certainly got the message from him that I was to be strong, not cry, or show fear – in other words to cover up feelings.

For instance, when I was a young teen in Wichita Falls, a man climbed in my bedroom window in the middle of the night, after carefully taking the screen off and leaning in against the house. I yelled for my dad, and the man got back out of the window and ran away. Minutes after that, my dad calmly nailed my window shut, only opening it a crack for air, and told me to go back to bed. Of course, I was scared, but did not dare voice it; I went back to bed in that same room minutes after the intruder had fled. The next day my dad hung a small fan on the wall near my bed, and that was that!

I hope you don't think this childhood perspective is over done. I think it was a necessary part of therapy – important to look at and then important to move on. I don't want to get caught in the blaming game; however, it makes sense that our early childhood experiences often plays a large part in forming who we are as adults. For me, this insight brought possible explanations; not necessarily earth shattering changes, especially involving weight loss. I will address that more later.

Chapter 7

October 1996, was upon me. I was getting nervous because I had decided to tell Dan toward the end of the month. I thought a few more therapy sessions would help me prepare. I had already seen the divorce attorney. Man, talk about weird. The day I picked up the phone and told him that I wanted to talk about a divorce was scary and rather sad. I never thought I would be using that word, "divorce." He was a nice, understanding man, and we worked well together; he was also very considerate of Dan's feelings.

I can't explain why I told people about my situation in the order I did – first John, then T.J., then Lory, then my therapist, then Dan. I know it's common for gays and lesbians to first tell someone they feel will be supportive and understanding. The sequence just seemed to fit. I felt I needed to be more comfortable with this news myself before telling Dan; I needed to be certain about it. By the way, I never had any guilt about being gay, I did fear hurting Dan and my son, Brad. As I have said many times, I dreaded breaking the news to PFLAG and the Dallas gay community. However, I was lucky to be able to come out in such a positive environment; I had been involved with PFLAG and the gay community for four years, and I knew to be gay was OK. Guilt about being gay was not a hurdle I had to face.

There were several events that had already been planned for October. Dan and Brad had their yearly dirt bike trip to New Mexico with their buddies at the first of the month. I flew to Washington, D.C to the National PFLAG

Convention the weekend of October 12th. It was a fun time. Cher was the speaker, and I got to say a few words to her after her speech. One of the things that stood out to me was a video that was shown at the first of the convention; it had random photos of families from the various chapters. One was a photo of Dan, T.J. and myself at the March on Washington. There we stood (Dan and I in our blue PFLAG T-shirts) with me holding my sign saying, "We love our gay and lesbian children.," and T.J. holding her sign saying, "We love our straight parents." I swallowed hard, knowing that soon that would no longer ring true for us.

The following weekend on Oct. 19th was the Dallas Black Tie Dinner, with Pat Schroder as the keynote speaker. Dan and I attended, he in his tux and I in a lovely new black dress. By that time I had lost 74 pounds. Of course, I hoped to see Lory there that night. I was about 15 pounds lighter than when she last saw me. We had talked a lot by phone; and I had sent her letters, letting her know how I was doing. However, we had not met in person since September 10th when I told her about my feelings. I had adjusted well to seeing her as my friend, my mentor, sort of a mother earth figure.

However, seeing her that night, set me back a little. I walked through the large dimly lit crowd, glancing around at the various tables, hoping to spot her. All of a sudden I looked up and Lory was right in front of me; we were face to face. We both sort of gasped in surprise. She seemed stunned to see me, probably stunned to see the weight loss. We hugged for what seemed a long time. She put her things down on her chair, turned around and grabbed my hands and held my arms out to look at me. She complimented me on how well I looked. That was Lory. She was always very affectionate and complimentary to all her friends. I knew that, but it was hard for me to not take it personally. Man, was I in high school, or what!

On Sunday, October 21, Dan and I had a PFLAG party at our place. About 60 people were there; in fact all nine tables on the decks were used, as well as some people sitting inside. Looking around our lovely home that night, I realized how I would miss my house at party time, with all those decks; however, it was time for others to have a turn at throwing the parties. Later in the evening I taught a few people to dance the Macarena, which was a lot of fun. That dance was very popular at that time, and I had taken some dance lessons at a local neighborhood studio. Even in our younger days, Dan didn't want to dance so I never learned. With most of my weight off and with the new realization, I was ready to try some new things.

On Tuesday, October 22, I gave a presentation at UT Southwest Medical Center to a class of Doctoral students, who were studying to be clinical psychologists. I so enjoyed doing those events, always hoping to make a difference regarding perceptions of gays and lesbians.

The following weekend of October 26th, included a PFLAG garage sale at my home, and a night out with John Selig to the gay and lesbian halloween celebration on Cedar Springs. Many straight people and their kids often attended as well. He and I spoke about my telling Dan in a few days; we both were nervous about it. Brenda had told me to have a friend by the phone the night I told Dan in case I needed them; John agreed to be standing by. There was no need of that, but I went along with it.

The reason I am going into some detail concerning my October 1996, schedule is because that particular time was very meaningful to me. I had planned for quite some time to tell Dan after all those events had passed; and as they were completed one by one, I became rather nervous. I knew my life would change rather abruptly, and I dreaded hurting Dan. I also knew that if he saw no alternative, we would move quickly toward a divorce. In fact, I mentioned that to Brenda when she asked how I thought things would go. She later told me that she was checking "my reality" by asking me that, trying to see if I had a handle on my situation.

I talked to Lory on October 28th; she was very uncomfortable about my telling Dan the next day. I had written her a letter, explaining that I would be honest with him, and I again explained my various feelings regarding her. I assured her that Dan would be sensible about it, that he would not blame her. She had done nothing. I felt I should be up front with him, including mentioning her name because he would better understand if he knew all the facts. I told Lory to stop feeling badly about my marriage or what I might lose concerning PFLAG and the gay community; she should not feel responsible in any way. I told her that my discovery of my orientation was real and that it did not hinge on her. I said she should be proud of what her appearance in my life had done for me. It also seemed clear that I had gotten comfortable in the gay community as I pursued my PFLAG work, so it was likely that my new realization was already bubbling under the surface.

I explained to her that I thought that one reason she was a catalyst for me was because I saw in her a lesbian who was also very sensual, and perhaps my subconscious ran with it. I wondered if I had hidden my sexuality with the weight because I thought to show it meant trying to attract men, and I didn't want that. Sorry, about the psychobabble. I guess when you get right down to it, the reasons don't really matter all that much. However, when a person goes through this big of an awakening in later life, there is bound to be a search for answers - at least at first.

At the end of our phone conversation, I asked Lory if anything in my letter had bothered her. She laughed with that great, throaty laugh of hers and said, "No, girlfriend, you have one sense of humor! I love reading your letters." She said that it was amazing, that my world was falling apart, and I was taking it so calmly. I told her that was because I had not yet told a lot of people. However, I was confident that I was doing the right thing in this situation. (Also, she only heard from the calm exterior.)

The day had finally arrived, October 29, 1996. Dan came home from work that evening, thinking that we were going out to a movie. When he walked through the den where I was sitting, I asked him to sit down, that I wanted to talk to him about something. I started out by saying that I thought I had the answer to why I had not been more affectionate during our marriage.

I quickly explained what had happened to me about two weeks after Lory spoke to PFLAG. I added that she did nothing to encourage me, that she had started a relationship with a woman who lived out of town. I assured him that I had not (or ever had) cheated on him. He seemed shocked when I said that I now saw myself as lesbian. He asked what I wanted to do; I asked him the same thing. He said that wasn't important, that I have had three months to think about this.

He asked if I wanted a divorce, and I said that was the only solution I saw since it involved an orientation issue. He said he would have our realtor come by soon to see what she thinks we could get for the house, and he told me to go ahead and file if I was sure of my feelings. That's the way it went: I filed the next day, and the "for sale" sign was in our yard the day after that!

I told Dan that I had first confided in John Selig, and that he had not encouraged me and was concerned that he (Dan) might have some animosity toward him. I said I had also told T.J. while we were visiting her, and that she had supported me, but was very concerned about him. He said that he did not have any ill feelings about Lory or John, that John should have known better than that.

I mentioned that Lory felt some unfounded responsibility and wanted to help me through this. Did he mind if she helped me find a place in north Dallas? He said "no," but asked if I was sure there was no relationship; I said there certainly was not a relationship going on, and we only communicated by phone. I reminded him that she was at the Black Tie Dinner with her girlfriend, and how out of sorts I had gotten with Lory when she kept canceling our lunch appointment. I had told him about that in regard to her helping me with PFLAG work. I explained that she was mainly a catalyst for my seeing my situation, a situation that I felt was always there; I had just not seen it. I told him that I was moving out with no one to go to, that I was prepared to live alone if need be.

There were no tears shed at that time; however, it became very sad later. It was beginning to sink in for both of us what was happening. I was very shocked when he began moving his things out of our bedroom to the guest room. I had not expected that. When he began moving things from his bathroom (located off of our bedroom) into the guest room bath, he said there was a lifetime of things in his bathroom cabinet. He added that he wouldn't have believed he would ever be doing this.

I called John, because I knew he was standing by and would want to know if things were OK. I told him it went well at first, and then Dan had moved to the guest room. I began to cry as I told him how sad Dan became when he was moving his things. John said, "It was harder than you thought it would be, wasn't it?" I said it was, but I still felt that I made the right decision and had no regrets. However, I felt badly for Dan and for the end of a 35 year marriage. I told John that Dan had no problems with him; John said to tell him that he loved him and for him to call to talk anytime.

I decided that I should go to Brad's house that night to talk to him about all of this. I knew Dan would be mentioning it the next day at work (Brad worked with Dan). My therapist had feared that telling them both the same evening might be too much for me, but I knew I needed to do it. As I was walking out our front door, Dan said, "You will have to bear with me for the next few days. This is just sinking in." I cried as I said, "I'm sorry." He told me to not blame myself.

I had called Brad before I left the house, telling him that I wanted to come over, that I had something to talk to him about. He later told me that he had immediately called T.J. to find out what was up; he was afraid someone had died. She said it had something to do with my relationship with Dan. When I walked into his den, I began to cry and finally said, "You are going to hate this; I asked Dan for a divorce tonight." I will never forget seeing Brad drop his head; then he looked up and asked, "Why?" I explained about Lory speaking and what followed later. He questioned me a lot about whether this was just an attraction to one woman; he wanted to be sure my therapist or others had not pushed me in that direction. He couldn't understand why I only realized I was lesbian three months ago. I explained the best I could.

He asked if I was sure I could be demonstrative with a woman, and was I sure I preferred women. I said yes to both. He said he will be concerned about his dad. By the end of our conversation, he said he needed to process everything, but that he hoped his dad and I both would eventually be happy.

When I returned home, Dan and I talked a little more. He asked me if there was any chance that this was caused by my medication, or a midlife crisis, or feeling like my life would soon be over. I said that I did not feel any of those things played a part. He mentioned that I was breaking our wedding vows. I suppose he meant by my not sticking to the "in sickness and in health, till death do us part." I explained that I felt this was a special circumstance, since I now had new information that I was not aware of when I was 18 and took those vows.

He agreed. I mentioned that he might find someone else and have a good relationship, that he deserved better than what he had with me. He said if not me, there will be no one. I hoped that would change.

He said he would talk to his coworker tomorrow about a recommendation for a lawyer.

As I prepared for bed that night, I found a sensitive note from Dan. In part, he asked me to not be concerned about him, that he would find a way of dealing with my leaving.

Chapter 8

On October 30 1996, I decided to tell one of my close friends; she had been battling cancer for two years. "Jessica" was someone I could count on, someone who would be honest with me. After I shared my story with her, she let me know that she wasn't surprised it was a woman, and she wasn't surprised it was Lory. She remembered my talking about her. Jessica said I had done nothing wrong, and that I deserved to have those special feelings. She asked me what was my worst fear in all of this. I said it was being out on my own and being lonely. She said that was OK, as long as it wasn't that I was not sure about my orientation. Everything else would fit into place. I said there may be people who will say that this was caused by my being around PFLAG and working with gays and lesbians. Jessica said no, that she could have done that, and she would not have become lesbian. She added that I was very brave to do this.

When I left her that day, we hugged and I told her thanks for being my friend for 26 years; and that she had better stay around, that I wasn't ready to say good-bye. She said she would. There were other friends who were not so supportive; they felt they had to take "sides" and were unable to support both Dan and myself.

The next person I felt needed to be told was my mom. Man, she had to face her only granddaughter being lesbian seven years prior, and now her only daughter was about to tell her the same thing. After I told her, she immediately said, "I still love you." However, it was obvious she was sad about losing Dan; she had thought so highly of him. I tried to assure her that I hoped we could re-main friends, and that she would still be able to see him. Mother, like many others, wanted to know if I was sure I was gay. In fact, the next day, she said she couldn't really believe I was gay, that it bothered her when she was alone thinking about it; but when she was with me, it seemed OK. She came along very fast with the situation, even pointing out articles in the newspaper about lesbi-ans getting AIDS as well as gay men (and how they could contract it). Too much information from my mom!

That day of October 30, 1996, was an intense one. Tell-ing friends and family was a very emotional ordeal, but a necessary process. That night I got a call from Brad. He wanted me to be sure and see down the road. I told him I had done that and could see possible problems of lone-liness, but I felt sure of my situation. He said he would miss our trips when he, Dan, and I flew to see T.J., the times that Brad and I played gin at the airports and on the plane. He also said he would miss our "Tuesday night dinners." We started those many years ago when T.J. lived in the Dallas area; we four would always get together for din-ner at our home every Tuesday evening. We continued them later - just the three of us. I told Brad that I thought we could still continue those things.

After talking to Brad, I asked Dan to not dismiss keep-ing our family together at least on some occasions; how-ever, I knew it was too soon for him to consider that. Dan made a comment that "if this can happen, anything can happen." I think this situation made him question a lot of things in life. I recommended that he read the book, *The Other Side of the Closet* by Amity Buxton, and I laid it out for him. The book addresses the challenges that spouses face when their husband or wife comes out as gay or lesbian.

I also laid out a video that his brother, Steve, had sent entitled, *Your Mom's A Lesbian, Here's Your Lunch: Have a Good Day at School*. The title is rather weird, but it's a warm and thoughtful story about Jane Spahr (a Presbyterian minister) who came out as lesbian to her husband, Jim, after 13 years of marriage and two sons. They divorced but have remained friends. The video opens with Jim toasting 30 years of friendship with Jane, friends and family in attendance. His current wife of 12 years is also shown.

Steve and his wife, Mary Ann, (and their two daughters) were among the very few examples of Dan's family that were able to support me as well as Dan. I so appreciated that (and still do).

I also encouraged Dan to go for counseling, but he said he did not believe that would be of any benefit to him. Living together in the same house during that short time was often stressful. We talked a little about the divorce settlement, and he said that he would be very fair with an equal split down the middle; he also said he would not get a lawyer that might take advantage of the lesbian angle.

Our little dog, Sandy, (a reddish poodle) didn't know what to make of Dan and me sleeping in separate rooms, because she had always slept on the end of our bed. She immediately began sleeping on my bed the first of the night, and then switched to his bed during the second part of the evening. Sad. It seemed that we were trying to quietly dodge each other in that big house. Well, I hoped that the worst and saddest part of this whole thing was behind me. Now I had to prepare to face informing PFLAG and the Dallas gay and lesbian community.

Chapter 9

Here it was the first part of November, 1996, and our Annual PFLAG meeting was coming up Thursday, November 14th; we would be electing officers at that meeting for 1997. The slate of nominees had already been sent out to the voting members, with my name listed as running for President and Helpline Vice President. This was to be my fifth and final year heading the organization, but now new information had arisen about me. I didn't feel it would make a difference, but in good conscience I could not keep this information from our voting members.

I quickly called a special board meeting at my house, telling each member that there was something of a personal nature I wanted to talk to them about. I had prepared a letter of explanation describing what had happened with me - a letter, with their permission, I wanted to mail out with our November newsletter. I had printed it on a light purple colored paper so that the reader would not miss it within their newsletter. I marked on the back of the fold: "PLEASE READ. THANKS!"

We board members sat around the table in Dan's study. I thanked them for coming and gave them a shortened version of what had happened to me. I did not mention Lory's name, and they did not ask. I ended with, "I now identify as lesbian; how does this affect PFLAG? One commented, "If we can't support you, what is PFLAG all about?" Dave said, "No one should be deprived of those feelings." Another member added, "You should now be even more qualified to be President." Ruth remarked,

"This doesn't sound like something that's happened just recently; it sounds like it's been there all along."

All members were supportive, but they were concerned about Dan and sad about the loss of us as a PFLAG couple. I told them that I had checked in with National PFLAG by calling the National President, Nancy McDonald. She was amazing. Her first comments were, "Now you will be able to see the gay and lesbian issue from two points of view, that of a parent and that of a gay person. You will just have to know which hat to wear, when, and where."

I read my letter from the purple sheet, and all members agreed that I should insert it in the newsletter. It would go to all members, plus others on our mailing list (including many gay and lesbians). It said:

An Important Personal Note From Pat Stone

President of PFLAG/Dallas

November 1996

"Some of you may feel this letter is unnecessary, and you may be right. Some of you may feel this letter only needed to go out to our Dallas voting members, and you may be right. However, those of you who know me, know that I am a very honest and open person – that I do not want anything that could be perceived as needed information to be hidden. Enclosing this with our newsletter is also an easy way to get this information to you, and perhaps those who are not our members will also have some interest.

Our next regular meeting is November 14th; it is also our Annual Meeting, and officers for 1997 will be elected. Our members have received a slate of these officers, and they will be voted on at that Nov. 14th meeting. I have been nominated for President as well as Helpline VP.

There has been a new development since I made the decision long ago to run for another year for these offices. I still plan to run for the offices, and I feel I am qualified for them and will do a good job. However, I want you to be aware of this new information before voting. It may not make a difference to you, but I want you to be informed.

I recently developed feelings for another woman. No relationship occurred between us – I am married and she is in a relationship. However, with therapy and much soul searching, I now see that this orientation was always there; I just did not see it before. I now identify myself as lesbian. This revelation explains many things; it is the missing piece of the puzzle that I have been working on for a long time.

I regret that this positive experience for me has led to much turmoil for my family – especially for my husband, Dan, and my son, Brad. My lesbian daughter, T.J., has had less stress over this, but I know she too is saddened by the future changes facing our family. Of course, none of them have a problem with the lesbian issue; however, they mourn the end of a marriage of 35 years.

My question to you is: does my being lesbian affect your feelings about my being President of PFLAG/Dallas and answering the helpline?

Please remember that first and foremost I am a parent of a lesbian daughter. In fact, our bylaws give only that as a requirement for Presidency – to be a parent of a gay, lesbian, or bisexual child.

I will not wear my orientation on my sleeve. My concern is fighting for equal rights for our kids and to help families accept their gay or lesbian loved ones. I am not going to be concerned about fighting for my rights at this point. I have had 53 years of heterosexual privilege so being concerned about myself is not my priority. I feel I am very effective on the helpline, and it is still very easy for me to talk to people as a mother of a lesbian daughter and as the President of PFLAG/Dallas. I do not feel that my orientation is a factor when talking to callers.

As I was going to announce at our next meeting, I had asked Dave Gleason almost a year ago (Jan. 1996) if he would consider running for President next Nov. 1997 – that I had always said after serving five years, I should step aside and let new leadership and new ideas surface.

I would remain active – perhaps in a newly created position. So this upcoming year would be my last year as President, and I have mixed feelings about that and will miss running the meetings. However, if Dave takes over, I know PFLAG/Dallas will be in good hands, and I will be near-by helping all I can. I hope you find this additional information helpful in making your decision. Please keep my family in your

thoughts; we all need your support. For those
who have already reached out to us, we
truly appreciate it.

Sincerely,

Pat Stone

President, PFLAG/Dallas

Our board meeting ended on a very warm and positive note. I later called Lory to tell her how things were
going. She had hesitated to call my home at that time
and had checked on me through John Selig.

The next day I called my friend and activist, Louise
Young, to give her a heads up on what had been happening with me. She was really happy for me; but said for
my sake, was I sure I wanted to continue as President of
PFLAG? I said yes, that I would hate to step down amid all
of this. The next day I got a call from one of the lesbians
who was a contact for PFLAG before we parents formed
the Dallas chapter. I will refer to her as "Cynthia" because
I don't believe she is out and she might not want publicity. She said she wanted to come by and talk, and that
she was bringing Louise Young with her (Cynthia's partner
also came, but did not share in the conversation).

I could tell when they walked in with grim faces that it
would be a serious visit. Dan and our dog, Sandy, went
to the guest room, and we four sat in the den. Louise
had second thoughts about the issue and was very concerned about how this would impact PFLAG and the
gay community. My worst, initial fears were coming true.
She and Cynthia felt I should seriously consider stepping
down from PFLAG. Louise said how she loved me and
Dan, and how much I had done to build PFLAG to what it
had become. However, she said that she would hate for

the right wing in Dallas to get hold of this and use it to hurt me and the PFLAG organization. She said they had done that to her and her partner many years ago.

Louise was also concerned about the media attention it would get. I told her that I couldn't believe this was that big of a deal; and she said it was a huge thing, maybe the biggest thing in the Dallas gay community for many years. She added that it could kill PFLAG. I bristled at that and replied, "Oh, Louise, PFLAG is stronger than that." I said I could handle the press, that nothing is worse than having someone attack your own child, and I had already faced that.

I told her about the time I was interviewed on an out of state radio show, and a guy referred to my daughter as an animal. I calmly told him that I was sorry he felt that way, that he just didn't understand the issues; if he knew my daughter, he would not feel that way. I had always been very careful to never stoop to the level of our attackers. By the way, several listeners called into the radio station, apologizing for the man who had been so rude.

I said to Louise and Cynthia that I would consider stepping down if I felt that the chapter would be at risk, but that I sure hated to knuckle under to what *might* happen. They told me that they had called my board members and several were now having concerns, but they were supportive of me and hated to see me step down. It was a very sad and tearful meeting. I remember tears rolling down my cheeks and Louise handing me tissues from her purse. She had only good intentions and was genuinely concerned for me and PFLAG; perhaps she was coming from past years when she was treated badly by the right wing. Before my guests left, I told them I would seriously consider the issues they raised.

Dan heard them leave and came into the kitchen to see what had taken place. I was in tears part of the time as I related their concerns. He said he hated to see me in such pain, and that he couldn't believe that he was counseling me while he was in such a mess. He said he had mixed feeling about the issues.

He asked if I wanted to go get something to eat; he said he never thought he would be able to do that. We went to one of our favorite Mexican restaurants, Mexacali. When we returned, Dan said he would definitely take a break from PFLAG, not just because of what was happening at that time. He sort of resented all the time I had devoted to it. (Brad had some of the same feelings about that). I suppose that was a natural reaction.

I continued to mull over the dilemma. My gut told me to fight it. I sure did not want my position with PFLAG to end this way. If I stepped down, I thought it would send a message that to be gay is not good. Our chapter could suffer more if there was not a well qualified person ready to step in. I did believe at that time that a chapter should be headed by a straight parent if possible, perhaps for the sake of the new parents coming in the door.

I thought I could manage for one more year, especially since I was still a parent, a parent whose child came out many years prior. I couldn't tell Lory about this until something was decided. I didn't want her to feel more responsibility or sadness over this. I think she thought I was making a big deal out of nothing when I mentioned this possible problem before.

The next day I called another respected activist, CeCe Cox; I also considered her a friend. She was the past president of DGLA (Dallas Gay and Lesbian Alliance). She had a different take on the situation; she said she didn't see a major problem, that she would only be concerned about the new parents. I agreed. I talked to Dave Gleason, and he said we shouldn't react too quickly due to a very few complaints. He was not ready to take over as president in 1997. I then faxed T.J.; in fact, I gave her all the details of the controversy and asked for her objective opinion.

Leave it to T.J. She came to my rescue once again with the perfect solution. She suggested that I serve out my last year as co-president, bringing in Dave Gleason (a straight Dad with a gay son) as the other co-president. I could do most of the work if that was what we decided, letting Dave get accustomed to being president the following year. T.J. added that if it was going to be a problem, I should seriously consider stepping down from the helpline if I could get a well qualified person to take it over.

I called Dave right away, and he said he would agree to being co-president. I called one of our moms and a board member, Martha England, and asked her to do the helpline. She was the mother of a gay son and a lesbian daughter, and she had been a counselor. Perfect. She said she would do it. To tell you the truth, I recently had second thoughts about continuing the helpline after a call I had received days ago. It was from a gay young man in east Texas. He shared the turmoil he had been having with his fundamentalist parents, and I talked to him as I had always done on the helpline – as a parent of a lesbian daughter. After our conversation, he said, "That's the most support I have ever gotten from a straight person." That made me feel somewhat dishonest.

I was happy to turn over the helpline to someone as qualified as Martha. I called the rest of the board, and they all approved of the new plan. I called Louise, and she also liked the idea. A few years later, she told me that she was happy that she had been wrong about her concerns. It takes a big person to say that. She also encouraged me to write a book about my experience.

As people began to receive their newsletters, our phone started ringing. Both Dan and I received several calls of support. All calls were positive with only one exception. Even that exception was from a woman who had genuine concerns. She felt things were moving rather fast, and I had to agree with that. Even if Dan had wanted to drag things out, I would have felt badly about keeping my orientation secret and letting members vote me in without all the facts. I could not have let that happen.

The woman was worried about what the Christian Coalition would make of this. I assured her that I didn't feel it would be a problem. Plus I figured they had bigger fish to fry than me and our Dallas chapter. How could any thinking person have an extremely hard time with this now that I was off the helpline and with us now having two presidents, one being a straight dad? We followed our bylaws and did everything by the book. Of course, that doesn't always mean things will go smoothly. Perhaps this would be a challenge for our chapter and it would benefit from the experience. It would test everyone; however I had never planned on being the center of such a test!

Chapter 10

The local gay and lesbian newspaper, *The Dallas Voice*, printed a story about the controversy in their November 15, 1996, issue. At press time they didn't have the result of the PFLAG election. The title of the article was: "PFLAG chief's coming-out sparks concern." Under that heading was: "President faces challenge in bid for re-election." It was written by reporter Tammye Nash.

It was an accurate piece, describing what had happened, the controversy, quotes from my letter to the members, and quotes from National PFLAG via Nancy McDonald. Nancy praised my contributions to PFLAG, both locally and nationally and said that "her moral stature and her positions on the issues will not change." She added, "PFLAG will embrace Pat as she has embraced others. Our main focus in PFLAG is to emphasize continued movement toward fulfilling our mission, and that takes all of us: parents, gays, lesbians, bisexuals – all of us. Nothing really changes" because of Stone's coming out.

The night had arrived. It was Thursday, November 14, 1996, and time for the PFLAG Annual Meeting. My mother came along with me that night. I was rather nervous because I wasn't accustomed to having the spotlight on my personal life. I was determined that the meeting would not dwell on that. It was my hope that the night would begin with "taking care of business," and then continuing with our regular PFLAG program. I had extra copies of my letter on the purple paper ready for anyone who had not received a copy. We had the sign-in sheet for all voting members. We had revised copies of the slate of officers that had been approved by the board. There were only two changes: Dave Gleason had been added to my name as Co-Presidents for 1997, and Martha England had replaced my name as running for VP Helpline. Those two positions were marked with an asterisk, noting that they represented a revision.

Soon after my words of welcome to our audience, I addressed our voting members; we had a large group that night, but there were only 50 voting members. I asked for a vote on the slate of officers; 48 voted for the slate with only 2 dissenting votes. The audience gave me a standing ovation, and the board presented me with a bouquet of flowers. I was so proud of and grateful for my board and our members – as well as National PFLAG. They all stood behind me and were willing to take a risk. By the way, Louise Young was there at that Annual Meeting and I was told that she voted for the slate of officers. I was proud of that. I was also told that the two dissenters were Cynthia and the woman I mentioned earlier. Someone who sat near them heard their "nay" vote. That's OK. There were no hard feelings on my part.

A note was given to me that night, along with the flowers. It was from the Board and Dave read it to the audience: "Dear Pat, The Board of PFLAG/Dallas take this opportunity to publicly thank Pat Stone for her devotion to this organization these past four years. If it had not been for her constant attention, PFLAG/Dallas would not be what it is today. She has been a role model for all of us – displaying courage, integrity and honesty. We are proud of Pat and her family. With love from, " (signed by all 9 board members).

On Nov. 17, 1996, I sent the board members a letter of thanks:

"The last few weeks have been rather tough for me, and I would not have made it through it without the support from you board members. There is no way I can thank you enough.

I sprang something on you that took a while to digest. I will always remember how concerned you were for me and Dan, as well as for the rest of my family, when I talked to you at that first board meeting. Supportive words came from you – one by one from around the table.

I know that some of you had additional concerns for PFLAG/Dallas after you recovered from the surprise and from the concern for me personally. That was to be expected, and I will never find fault with that. You will remember that my words were: 'I now identify as lesbian; how will this affect PFLAG?'

However, after thinking about those concerns and airing them at the second board meeting, you decided we could overcome the possible problems – that there was no reason for me to step down as President. I thank you for that.

As a board we showed strength and determination to stand up for what is right; yet, we were wise enough to make a couple of changes in order to accommodate our new parents and families. I feel we handled this situation in a responsible fashion, and I also feel we can handle any future repercussions. Thanks again. Sincerely, Pat Stone"

Several gay and lesbians told me that in their community some had to look at internalized homophobia in respect to my coming out. However, I think it was more than that. They saw me as a straight parental advocate and hated to lose that, and they also admired Dan and dreaded losing us as a PFLAG couple. In addition, they were very protective of our PFLAG chapter.

I held no grudges against those few who reacted negatively to my news; most were very supportive and flooded me with understanding cards and letters. There were some people, both gay and straight, who could not understand why I was so certain that I was lesbian considering the fact that I had not acted on my new found orientation. However, straight people are rarely questioned as to whether they are really straight when they have not yet acted on it. I feel my story showed that to be gay or lesbian did not hinge completely on sex. It's what is in a person's heart, and who they are attracted to.

Many people complimented me on how courageous I was to be so forth coming. I didn't see it that way, because it was the only way I could have done it. There was no other choice. When Lory read the purple sheet in the newsletter, she called me and again with that great voice said, "Girlfriend, you are going to be one great lesbian, because you've got balls!" I loved the compliment, but as I said, there was no other way for me to have handled it.

I chose to keep Lory's name out of the letter and out of all the press. She told me that it was my decision, that if it would help explain the story to go ahead and use her name. However, I decided she did not need that at the time, especially since she felt some undeserved responsibility.

On November 22, 1996, Tammye Nash of *The Dallas Voice* did a follow up story entitled, "PFLAG chapter re-elects Stone." Under that heading was, "Recently-acknowledged lesbian enters 5th term; Gleason co-president." It mentioned the 48 to 2 vote, that Martha England would take over the helpline, the bouquet of flowers and the standing ovation.

I wondered if Mayor Kirk or Steve Blow from the *Dallas Morning News* had seen or heard about the two articles in the *Dallas Voice*. Both men had been very supportive of gay and lesbian rights in Dallas. I hoped they would be understanding of my situation.

Some of us PFLAG parents met Steve Blow back in 1993, when there was some unrest as the Dallas City Council debated the Police Department's ban on hiring gays (a ban that was soon lifted). Many people showed up at City Hall wearing stickers saying, "No Homo Cops." They claimed to be "pro family" and even brought their children decorated with those horrible stickers. Steve wrote a column about that disturbing scene and interviewed PFLAG parents in regard to it. I admired Steve for taking a stand, and I mailed him our Christmas card the following year.

It was a picture card of our family, which included our new grandson. Dan wrote a powerful letter that accompanied the photo, introducing our lesbian daughter and grandson to our friends and family. Steve printed portions of it in his *Dallas Morning News* column on Sunday, December 11, 1994, entitled "A father's wish at Christmas is for tolerance." A brief excerpt from that column:

> "When T.J. told us several years ago that she was a lesbian, I was surprised. I was also very ignorant about what it meant. At that time I didn't think I knew any gay people. Since then, I have found out that I knew far more than I realized. You probably know a lot of gay folks. They often keep it secret because they don't know how their family and friends will accept the news (or them). That's a shame, isn't it?...
>
> I hear hateful messages from some of the current religious leaders, and it offends me. That's my wonderful daughter they're talking about. And the descriptions they use of gay people are so terribly inaccurate. Like dead fish, messages of hate still stink, even when wrapped in pages from the Bible.

Think about it, what if those religious leaders are simply wrong? They've been wrong before. Others of their cloth were wrong about the Jews and the Blacks and the Catholics and the Native Americans, about almost anyone else who was different...Won't they be surprised when St. Peter asks why they were so unaccepting of some of God's children?...

I hope you get the message. It's one that shouldn't be put in the closet. It needs talking about. I care about what you think or I would never have sent you this letter. I love my daughter, and I admire her. I accept her without any reservation, and I want you to accept her and her family with the warmth that you have always extended to me.

That's my Christmas wish.

Happy Holidays, Dan."

Dan gave our chapter his permission to make copies of his complete Christmas Letter, and it became a prized handout for our PFLAG parents and for gays and lesbians as well.

Chapter 11

It began to leak out among some in the gay and lesbian community about Lory being the catalyst for my coming out. Guess what comment I began to hear? That I was not her type! *Type*? What was all of this about *type*? The word was that Lory preferred younger, butch women. I knew that she and I would not make it in a relationship, but to be rejected because I was not butch? I was not happy about that whole butch/femme thing. I understand it better now; but at the time, I was appalled that there would be lesbians, of all people, who would discriminate against me! I am told that the butch/femme situation was more common years ago than at the present time. Lory wouldn't address it with me; she just said it was more of an "attitude" thing with her. I wondered what happened to being attracted to someone for their ethics, their sense of humor, even their good looks, etc. I know I was naïve. I began to hear things like, "butch on the streets, but femme in the sheets." Guess I had a lot to learn.

I didn't know if I had a *type*; everything was very new to me. I did know that even many straight people preferred certain types or specific characteristics in their partners. I remembered Lory describing herself as a "butch in drag" when she spoke at PFLAG in July. I suppose that meant that she had the attitude of a butch, but dressed as a femme – a very confusing message for some of us. I hoped there would be someone out there who would see me as their *type*, as well as like me for my inner worth.

I was too old to change. I was going to continue to wear lipstick, polish my nails, and carry a purse!

It was too soon to seriously consider dating anyone. I was still married and still living at home with Dan. I buried myself in my PFLAG work – answering the helpline (until Jan. 1997), preparing packets of literature for new parents, arranging speakers, speaking at functions, etc. I also spent time getting our house ready to be sold. Dan and I had to go through our things, deciding what to keep, who wanted certain things, what to put into a garage sale. It was a sad and tedious ordeal, going through 35 years of memories. He typed a list of all of our furniture, and we made our own decisions concerning our possessions. We were very fair with one another, and our lawyers cooperated with what we decided.

T.J. flew in to spend some time with us at Thanksgiving, and on November 27, 1996, she and Brad joined me in a therapy session with Brenda. Even though they were in their early 30's (T.J. 33 and Brad 30), their parent's divorce was a sad thing for them. I thought it might be helpful for the three of us to talk together about it. I will just touch on a few things, since some comments were meant to be part of a private therapy session.

Brad had a few issues. He knew our marriage wasn't perfect; but he said if there was to be a divorce, he thought it would be after much counseling and more time devoted to trying to save the marriage. I felt that with an orientation issue, extra time and couple counseling didn't seem to be the answer for us.

An additional concern for Brad was the fact that I seemed too concerned about how PFLAG and the gay community would react to my being lesbian. I could understand his feelings on that. I explained that I often voiced my concern over that issue, but I didn't mean it was more important than the hurt that would be felt by his dad. However, I did have great sadness at the loss of my *voice* with PFLAG and the gay community. There was still much work to be done in changing misconceptions about gays and lesbians, and I wanted to be part of it.

T.J. said she had seen problems within the marriage years ago. She and Brad talked about what good parents Dan and I had been, that I had been a great mom – being their scout leader, their room mother, etc. T.J. and I cried several times. Brenda felt it was beneficial that everyone had a chance to air their thoughts and concerns. I felt it was good that Brad was able to hear things from my perspective. I hesitate to use the word *side* because there were no *sides* to this; there was no fault or anyone to blame. Perhaps that was what made things so difficult. In fact, Dan once commented, "You are leaving me for no one." I didn't see it as leaving him, as much as leaving the situation due to new information. I truly believed he deserved better, and I felt I had handled things with honesty and I hoped with sensitivity.

When we returned home from therapy, T.J. helped me sort through some things, especially upstairs in her old room and in our attic. I told her to take anything that meant something to her. I was surprised at one of her choices – our "sunshine sheets." Years ago when she and Brad were little kids, we lived in a smaller place that had a clothes line in the back yard. I often hung out all of our sheets, and referred to them as "sunshine sheets" due to that special smell they absorbed from hanging outside. She recently told me that she still has them and can almost smell that fragrance to this day.

The four of us (T.J., Brad, Dan, and myself) had Thanksgiving dinner at my mom's house that year. Her husband, "Sam," was also there. We all went through the motions, but things were very awkward. Usually our family joined our friends at our east Texas land referred to as *Brushyland* for an outdoor Thanksgiving, but that was not to be that year.

One evening after returning home from an appointment, Dan met me at my car and said that he did want to remain friends; I said that I did also, that we had always been friends. He seemed to be doing better, his voice friendlier. He even remarked that I looked like I was still losing weight. I was hopeful that things were looking up.

Dan was right; I was still losing weight – a total of 96 pounds, and I had stopped the Phen-Fen medications a few weeks prior. I continued eating smaller portions, and I kept up with my daily calories and fat count. I also continued to exercise and work out. Dan and I had agreed years ago that if I ever got the weight off, I would need surgery to correct the loose skin; we planned for the money to be there for that. Now it was time. I know the timing of the surgery seems strange; however, the expense was taken into consideration during the divorce settlement.

I can tell you that one of the worst things for the elasticity of the skin, besides the sun, is to continually gain and lose weight, which I did over and over again. I was lucky enough to have my mom's youthful genes; she always looked at least 10 to 15 years younger than her years. If I had maintained my weight as she had, I doubt that cosmetic surgery would have seemed so necessary.

In early December of 1997, I had that tummy tuck that I mentioned earlier, in which 9 pounds was removed (Now I had a loss of 105 pounds!), and I had a breast lift. Those two surgeries were done at the same time. Several weeks later, I had a face lift. All surgeries went well, with no complications. I hardly had any discomfort at all from the tummy tuck or breast lift; I took no pain pills after I came home, so I was driving in a couple of days.

By the way, I had the breasts of a twenty year old! With the face lift, I had some minor stinging on my upper eye lids. Have you seen people who gain a lot of weight, but their face does not get fat? Well, that is not me. My face gets so heavy with additional weight, and upon losing it, I am left with a lot of sagging skin.

I moved in with my mom during the surgeries so she could help me take care of the bandages, the drains, etc. I will always remember her sitting with me at the hospital before the doctor did my tummy tuck. She watched as he drew lines on the fat and skin to be removed. She said, "Patsy, you should have had that done long ago." She was very sympathetic. There's nothing like having a supportive mom. I don't know what I would have done without her, then or on many other occasions.

As I continued to recover from the surgeries before the Christmas holidays, I had some emotional down times. I told Brenda, my therapist, that I was having some mixed feelings. On the one hand, I was rather excited about getting out on my own and learning more about myself. Like many women from my era, I came from living with my parents to living with my husband; this would be the first time to be out on my own. I told Brenda that I knew there would be some sad and lonely times. She said that would be OK as long as I let myself grieve at those times. She said it would not mean that I made the wrong decision; it would just mean that some things would be missed.

I remembered hearing people say how they feared being old and alone, perhaps in ill health. Dan could die of a heart attack at any time (like my Dad), and I would be alone. I could die of a heart attack tomorrow. So why plan my life on what *might* happen? I was sure there were many older women out there surviving on their own. It might not be the best of situations, but it could work. I was only 53 years old, and I hoped to have many years left. It was important to me to live my life honestly.

I told Brenda that I would not be looking for a relationship right away, that I wanted to get more in touch with myself first. She said that was when you usually find someone, that a woman might come along that I would have interest in, and the feelings would be very intense. That was enticing and scary at the same time.

Dan and I were to attend the December 1996, meeting of DGLA (Dallas Gay and Lesbian Alliance) to receive their Board of Directors Award. What an honor. They had heard about the divorce and decided to give us individual awards. Unfortunately, I still had drainage tubes and staples, but Dan said he would go that night to receive his award. I was surprised and happy about his decision, and I hoped it was an important turning point.

He accepted his award and told the audience that the main reason he came was to clear up any possible misconceptions from the media that he had a problem with PFLAG or the gay community over this personal situation. He said he did not, and he added some nice things about me. Many people told him how brave it was for him to do that; and by my not being there, I think people felt freer to come up to him and chat. Texas Representative, Harryette Ehrhardt, was there and spoke to him several times; she also received an award that night. She was quite a friend of PFLAG, a straight woman who has always been supportive of gay issues. She was one of our outstanding speakers at PFLAG, and I still consider her a friend. She was so supportive and understanding of the situation between Dan and me. By the way, I received my award a few months later, along with Louise Young and Vivienne Armstrong.

The media coverage had lessened with the exception of three small articles. National PFLAG sent out a press release on November 27, 1996, applauding the "Roseanne Show" for showing gay and lesbian issues as typical family dialogue. Their Thanksgiving dinner featured a gay couple discussing adopting a child, and Roseanne's mother inadvertently came out of the closet as a lesbian. The press release also included a quote from me describing my recent journey.

The Washington Blade's November 29, 1996, edition picked up on my story as well and printed it under their National News section entitled: "PFLAG leader comes out as Lesbian." "Stone's revelation marks the first time an acting chapter president has come out, although gays head up many of PFLAG's 400 chapters, said Nancy

McDonald, PFLAG's national president. This underscores an incredible need for us all to work together to address homophobia."

There was an article in the *Dallas Morning News* on December 24, 1996, entitled "Hotline opened to support gays who come out during holidays." The article mentioned that it was common for gays and lesbians to come out to their parents over the holidays, and that they, as well as their parents, should call the PFLAG hotline if things do not go well. It included several quotes from me and also mentioned that my daughter had come out about 8 years prior, and that I realized in July that I was lesbian also.

I hope you don't get bored with my mentioning the media coverage, but I want you to have the sense of what it was like coming out amidst the publicity; it was rather strange since I had not even acted on what was being discussed. I did not seek out the stories, but I was happy to cooperate, thinking that perhaps I would reach other women out there who were going through similar experiences. It looked like there was more coverage around the corner. But first, it was time to get through the holidays.

Chapter 12

On December, 20, 1996, I gave Dan the following letter:

"Dear Dan,

I am not sure what I want to say in this letter. I guess the main thing is to say how sorry I am that the new information about myself has caused you so much pain. I also regret the pain it has caused Brad as well.

I want you to know that our 35 years of marriage have not been all bad for me; I think you know that. I do not regret those years. We have two unbelievable children and a lot of good memories from those years.

I do appreciate the things you gave me – financial as well as non-financial. You were my provider, my friend, and my protector. I already miss those things, and I miss the little things we did such as playing with Sandy, going to movies, going out to eat (especially our Saturday Schloskeys). I miss our work together at PFLAG and the interaction we had with T.J. and Brad. I even miss playing games at Mema's and Sam's.

Even though I miss all those things, I know the divorce is the right thing to do in this situation.

I am still sure about my orientation even though I am not leaving to be with a particular woman. So to stay in the marriage would not be fair to either of us. I do fear being lonely and alone as I am sure you do also.

But I do not see any other way. Hopefully in time we will both find someone to share our life with; if not, I hope we can find happiness alone. It is also my hope that we can be friends; I don't think you believe this can happen, but perhaps you will change your mind in time. Please help me keep our family together as best as we can. Others have done it, and I know we can too. I don't think I have to explain that I did not do this on purpose to hurt you.

I think you know that this new awareness seemed to come to me out of the blue in July. I guess it was coming to the surface for the last few years. It kills me to see you so sad and to see you trying to avoid me – and avoiding being with our family. Now you say you are going to leave town rather than be with us during the holidays. I guess you have to do what you think you need to do. I hope you change your mind.

Please do not take this as a personal rejection. When an orientation issue is involved, it's a different situation. I know that may be hard for you to see now. I want you to take care of yourself – mentally and physically. You are still the father of our children and grandfather of our grandchild. We all care about you. Do the things you have always wanted to do.

Again, I am sorry for the pain. This has got to
get better with time. Just don't pull away
completely from me and the kids.

I will always remember the good times.

Love, Pat"

Dan said he appreciated the letter. I felt it might be
a type of closure for me, and I was hopeful that it would
help Dan better understand what had happened. As I
stated in the Preface, it's hard for me to share my story
with you without bringing Dan into the picture. I have
tried very hard to not get too personal in presenting our
situation. In fact, I left out the more personal comments
that were in the letter I just shared with you. I don't want
to make him feel uncomfortable, but I want my account
to be an honest one. It's a hard line to walk.

Dan did leave town during the holidays. Mother, Sam,
and I went to Brad's place for Christmas Eve. We had a
good time; I brought Brad's favorite fudge, and Mother
brought his favorite lemon pound cake. We opened presents, played with his cat, Tiger, and admired Brad's new
fish aquarium. It was unlike any Christmas past or future,
but we enjoyed our time together. The next day, Mother
and Sam went to his family for Christmas Day, and Brad
and I had lunch at a Chinese restaurant – one of the few
places open on that day. So we all made it through the
holidays.

It was time to pack away the few Christmas decorations I had put out that year. I looked through our Christmas cards one more time, reading the nice notes that
many included regarding the divorce. One was from a
friend and neighbor from our past house. She thanked us
for our part in her daughter's childhood and mentioned
how much she and her husband appreciated our agreement to be their daughter's guardian if something had

happened to them. She ended with, "I wish you both the best as you do what you have to do. I'm on both your sides as you travel this rocky road. My heart and our door is always open to each of you."

An additional note caught my eye; it was from my friend, Mary, who attended UTD (University of Texas at Dallas) with me in the late 1970s. We had a lot of fun in those literature classes. She and her husband and Dan and I went out to dinner a couple of times, and she and I continue to keep in touch. I will always value her support. Her note was to me and ended with, "I know this is a most difficult time for you and your family, but I have all kinds of confidence in your family and I know you will all survive this stronger than ever. I hope you find the partner of your dreams; and failing that, I hope you learn to live blissfully alone learning all about yourself – now that you are facing yourself fully. Good luck. Mary"

Unfortunately, I had saved a letter from the close relative I spoke about earlier – the one who never mentioned my daughter's name to me after she came out as lesbian. She was very negative about my situation. The letter was bad enough, but the booklet she sent was sad and ridiculous. She did not even include who wrote it, but she highlighted: "We do not hate gays, but we strongly DETEST the goals and life styles of homosexuals and lesbians; deeply DETEST their attempts to infect the minds of our children and grandchildren with Satan's perversions!" She knew that description did not fit me or T.J. Where was her heart?

Before I put the lid on the last box of decorations, I added a note dated "Christmas 1996," and it said: "Where will I be, who will I be with (if anyone), and what will be my mood when I unpack these things next Christmas?" I did not know it at the time, but that started a tradition with me. Since that day, I have written a note at the end of each year and inserted it into the box of Christmas decorations. Eventually it became a synopsis of what had happened during that year.

The New Year of 1997, came in without fanfare at our home. Dan and I were disappointed that our house had not yet sold, but we knew November through January was not the best time to sell. In addition, the real estate market wasn't doing so well at that time. I no longer presided over PFLAG/Dallas; but I continued to attend most of the meetings, and I was still a board member. Dave Gleason was doing a fine job. As I had hoped, there were no repercussions regarding my coming out and our handling of the situation.

Dave invited me to speak with him at a meeting of future school principals. He thought it would be effective to have the voices of both a mom and dad, plus the voices of the current president of PFLAG and one of its founders and it's former president. I had to decide if I should refer to my recent coming out. I wanted to be honest, but decided that would not add anything to our presentation. It was not about me; it was about encouraging the future principals to be understanding in regard to the gay and lesbian students. Dave and I gave our presentations and then opened the floor to questions.

After about the fourth question, a man asked if we had ever had the situation where one of our parents came out as gay? My heart skipped a beat; Dave glanced at me, giving me a chance to decide if I wanted to answer. I told the audience that I had to be honest with them and briefly told them my story. I mentioned that this had been a very recent occurrence and apologized if my voice sounded a little shaky. As Dave later said, "You could have heard a pin drop" during that section of my presentation. He said it caught them off guard, since they had seen me as a straight mom; and I did not fit their stereotype of a lesbian. From all outward appearances, they were very understanding, and many came up to me afterward, saying they had enjoyed hearing my story.

I began to miss my *voice* with my local chapter, but perhaps I would find it in another area. Later in the year I became Southern Regional Director of PFLAG, and I was elected to the National Board, which was based in Washington, D.C. Both positions were a real honor for me, but I preferred the work at the grassroots level.

The Dallas Voice printed a lengthy story on January, 17, 1997, entitled "PFLAG president-turned-lesbian is facing sweeping lifestyle changes." Under that title was, "Romantic feelings for another woman led Pat Stone to question her orientation and 35 – year marriage." Reporter, Thomas Rockman, came to my house for the interview, and he did a good job with the story. He went into more detail than past articles, giving more background history, describing specific paintings that I had done, and explaining my reason for the interviews. For instance, one of my quotes that he included was, "I see more married women coming out as lesbians. If I can help them in any way then my whole coming out publicly is worth it." He mentioned that I would be looking for a townhouse or condo, a place with white walls, something light and airy – with no southwestern influence, no dark paneling (like I had at the present time). He ended the article with, "There were some good times here, but I wasn't really here," she says, looking at the "For Sale" sign stuck in her front yard. "It's hard to put into words...I wasn't connected. Only a part of me was here."

On January 20, 1997, T.J. and I had a fun excursion. It was an emotional relief for me to get away for a few days. We went to President Bill Clinton's Inauguration! I had received an invitation, and decided to ask her to go with me. We couldn't afford the expense of the hotels in Washington, D.C. because the prices were jacked up for the event, plus we decided to not stay over night anyway. We drove from her place, took the rail outside of D.C, dressed in our casual clothes. We then attended the Inaugural Parade, where we were able to see the Presidential limo. Bill and Hillary even stepped out of the limo and walked for a while.

When we arrived at the fancy hotel, we took our formal clothes into the bathroom, changed and emerged looking very elegant. I have pictures of T.J. going through the bathroom door dressed in travel clothes, and coming out of the bathroom door in her sequins. We checked our old clothes at the hotel, and we were set to go. What a fun trip. Of course, one of my most favorite parts was when we were on the rail system, and someone asked if we were sisters! That was a first for me, and it was well deserved because of all the times that my mom and I were taken for sisters. I would have never been mistaken for my daughter's sister if I had not lost that 100 pounds. Excuse the vanity, but I had spent a lot of years being really large.

When I arrived back home, I learned that my divorce had become final on January 17, 1997. The process had taken less than three months. It became even more strange as Dan and I continued to live together, but separate, in our house.

I received a call from a very professional reporter from the *Dallas Observer*, Ann Zimmerman. She wanted to do an in depth cover story on my coming out. I decided the paper could reach a lot of women that might be sharing my experience, so I agreed to the interview. The article appeared on January 30, 1997, and it was called "Late Bloomer." Ms Zimmerman was very fair and understanding concerning the subject matter. There were a couple of things that in hindsight seemed rather personal, but I don't think Dan took offense. He said he was not upset with the article, but that he would be glad when all the publicity was over.

In general, the article was very complimentary; but to be fair, I will share with you the one negative comment made (anonymously, of course):

"To change your whole life based on some feelings you haven't had the chance to try out, it's nuts, especially at her age and situation in life," says a lesbian who has known Pat for years through her active membership in PFLAG. "Where is she going to meet people? I think she is being a little Polyanna-ish. I think she might be more isolated that she realizes. It's not like she's becoming part of a large cohesive club. And it's not like a bunch of politically active lesbians have offered her support."

T.J had several good quotes, but I especially liked the ones which closed the article:

"Whatever was going on in that marriage, it was something my dad counted on. It was very much how he defined himself," says T.J. "This has thrown him off balance. But I have confidence he can figure out the next chapter of his life, too. With my mom, I am concerned about the backlash that can happen to anyone as open and honest as she is. It appears she's made a lot of changes fast, but there was a substantial incubation time. She spent a lot of time thinking there was something unexplored inside of her. For the most part, I think she is pretty courageous. She is making the kind of changes you want people to make – a leap to what makes her feel more congruent with who she is. She got to the point that what she was doing didn't fit anymore.

She made changes pretty boldly. She considered not (changing), but I think she realized the price of not doing it would get to be too high."

There is no way I can explain to you how strange it was to see myself on the cover of that newspaper, especially when I saw the papers in those coin operated stands on the sidewalks. I started out as just a little farm girl from Wichita Falls, Texas, and was a stay at home mom (an important job). I don't mean that I came off as Madam Curie, but the article did go into all the work I had done through PFLAG, fighting for equal rights for my daughter and other gays and lesbians. I was proud of that time in my life. Of course, the article also went into some detail regarding my coming out and its repercussions. I was hopeful that by sharing that, I would be able to help other women out there.

And that was what happened. I received many phone calls, some letters, and an email from a woman in Austin, Texas. Her brother who lived in Dallas, sent her the paper. She had a similar story; she was age 42 and had come out two years prior after 15 years of marriage and three children. She said, "That *Observer* article was a good reminder that I need to attend a meeting of the local (Austin) chapter of PFLAG."

A reaction that I had not expected came from a gay man who emailed me saying that the article helped him identify with what his family and friends will have to deal with after he comes out to them. He said it also strengthened his belief that he needed to share with them, as much as possible, what he had been feeling and going through all those years when he was not yet able to admit to them or himself that he was gay.

The *Dallas Observer* printed the following letter on February 20, 1997:

"I must commend you on your sensitive handling of a socially taboo subject. Many people are upset when a previously married woman with children comes out of the closet to follow her own inner leanings. She no longer fits into a neat and tidy stereotype. Pat Stone is to be praised for her courage and honesty. She

proves that homosexuality goes far beyond the
sex issue. Perhaps in a more enlightened time,
she would have realized her true self sooner. But
I believe she'll have the best of both worlds. I
do have compassion for those who feel the hurt
of her recent revelation. There are more of you
than you might suspect, and several sources
of group support for the straight partners who
have been left. I write from experience, as I was
also the lesbian in a marriage that wasn't working because of my sexuality. Thanks again for
bringing us out of the closet." Gail from Dallas

After receiving numerous calls from women looking
for support in this area, I decided to start a social/support
group called "Late Bloomers." It did not seem appropri-
ate to meet in the house that Dan and I were sharing,
so I talked to him about my moving out. It looked as if
it would be a while before our house sold. He felt that
would be a good idea and said he could handle the sale
of the house.

Chapter 13

I, with Lory's help, began looking for a place. I wanted to be in north Dallas, close to the location of PFLAG, and that area would not be too far for my mom to drive to visit me. Lory and I had a lot of fun checking out several places; she was very patient, taking time to help me mentally place my furniture. We eventually found the perfect spot, a lovely two story townhouse near Midway Road, LBJ, and Forest. It had 2600 sq. ft. compared to my former house with almost 5,000 sq. ft. But who needs that much space, especially for one person – or even for two people? This would be great.

There were three bedrooms upstairs, a den, living room, dining room, and kitchen downstairs. There were two baths upstairs and a half bath downstairs – plus a utility room and an attached garage. It was light and airy, with white walls! There was even a small fenced courtyard for Sandy – plus a large communal area outside of that so I could still entertain. Perfect! My first home of my own. I couldn't wait to move in. It seemed like such a nice, safe and quiet neighborhood – right in the heart of "Loryland." The name came from the fact that Lory sold to many gays and lesbians in that area.

As Lory took care of all the paperwork regarding the townhouse, I began making arrangements to move. I was better able to concentrate now that the media coverage was finally over. There were only two recent articles. One was a guest editorial that I wrote for *Spectrum*, a gay and lesbian publication, entitled "Coming Out." The other was an article in the National PFLAG newsletter, entitled "PFLAG Dallas President Comes Out." Both were in their March 1997 issues. The PFLAG article included a nice photo of T.J. and myself.

I had given a copy of the *Dallas Observer* to Elizabeth Birch, Executive Director of HRC (Human rights Campaign) while she was in Dallas. I had the pleasure of chatting with her at various PFLAG and HRC events, and I admired her very much. She sent me a nice letter in response:

"Dear Pat:

Thank you for sharing with me the *Dallas Observer* article about your coming-out. It was an incredibly well-written article, and I was touched by the story of your journey. Best wishes to you and your new "Late Bloomers" support group. Keep on doing the very fine work that you are doing on behalf of gay and lesbian Americans. It is very appreciated. And please keep taking the time to take care of yourself in your new adventure.

Sincerely, Elizabeth Birch"

I was looking forward to having another meeting with my "Late Bloomers." The calls continued to come in from women who had read the *Observer* article. I offered them support by phone and told them that our next meeting would be in my new home in March. In fact, my moving date was March 3, 1997.

In the meantime, it was time to pack up my things. Dan and I went through the framed photos that were displayed in our den, and we decided who wanted what. We had already split most of our other possession between us. I was happy that he had taken the large oil painting that I had done of his grandfather playing dominoes and the smaller painting I had done for his dad - a still life of the Quaker Oats box sitting by a sugar bowl, creamer, a bowl of oats, a spoon and napkin. His dad ate Quaker Oats every morning for breakfast.

I had to decide what to take and what to put into a garage sale. Since I was moving to a townhouse, I figured I didn't need so much cookware; and besides, I didn't think lesbians did a lot of cooking. Man, did I later regret getting rid of so much of my "stuff!" However, I enjoyed putting my "fat clothes" in the garage sale.

Going through some of my old spiral notebooks in my desk drawer, I found sad reminders of my struggles to lose weight through out the years. They were pathetic and rather embarrassing, and they were a testimony of hopelessness. All the notebooks were similar in style, just the dates and weights varied. I always made charts for weight loss: a column for current date, current weight, a space for amount lost for that week and a space for total loss. If I was really into that particular diet, I also had columns for my measurements – bust, waist, hips, thighs, calf, and ankle.

The heading always included the diet I was on at the time, and usually an event that I wanted to attend after the weight loss, like a cruise with our friends. Sometimes I included embarrassing notes declaring I would be successful *that* time. There were pages after pages, notebook after notebook of those records. The weight would go down, then back up. I would stop that diet and try another diet. I could see that many pounds were added each time. I threw all of it away, hoping I would never have to resort to that again.

T.J. and I have often laughed about one particular diet program I was on where I had to write down who I was eating with; often I was eating with her. I believe it was the old Shick program where the "counselor" gave me a slight shock as I ate my favorite food (candy bars). I was allowed to take a bite of the bar, chew it, then spit it out. Needless to say, I was able to figure out that if I ate candy bars at home, I would not be shocked, nor would I have to spit them out.

As I was cleaning out the drawers in my closet, I found an old letter that T.J. had written August 3, 1989, when she was 25 years old; it was addressed to "Mom, Dad, & Brad." It was a letter she left with us as she was about to drive away from our house and from Dallas, headed to a new state and a new relationship. She had recently come out as lesbian and was about to strike out on her own. I couldn't believe I was reading that letter as I was about to do the same. You sure don't understand a person's situation until you walk in their shoes. I now *felt* things that I thought I *knew* before.

Her car was loaded and she was on her way to our place to say "good-bye." In the letter she wrote about the tears she had shed, how she had gone by the gas station that we had used for 20 years and told the men, "You guys take care of my family, OK?" She had looked around our old neighborhood and saw the Pizza Hut that she and Brad had walked to as kids and saw Gingham Girl Dance Studio where she took dance for so many years. She remembered the "security of the home" we had created for her, and the fact that she had never been away from her "family's familiar faces" for longer than 1 ½ weeks. However, she felt like the next step was right for her. She ended the letter with, "I guess strong will, your support, and my own pioneer spirit will keep me from kicking and screaming as I pull out of your driveway. I love you all very much! I'll call you tonight. Love, T.J./ Tammy" (Brad still calls her Tammy.)

Rereading that letter at the time I was about to make such a change was significant for me. I saw how the change she was about to make was sad for her, but she knew it was the right decision. She looked back at her past and cherished it with no regrets, but she was ready to move on in a different direction. It reminded me of the quote from Susan Taylor: "In every crisis there's a message; it's nature's way of forcing change. It's breaking down old structures so something new and better can form."

About a week before I moved, I asked Brad and my friend, Jessica, to come by and see the townhouse and meet Lory. The meeting went really well, and they loved the new place. Since Jessica was an interior designer, she had some ideas for me; and she later went with me to pick out some wall paper for the bathrooms. I was so happy that she felt well enough to become involved in my new home. I think it was a welcome distraction for her.

Mother had already seen the townhouse, and was sure she would be able to drive there to see me. I know she was rather sad about my moving from her neighborhood. I promised I would still come by almost every day to pick her up and go for lunch and our work out (I kept that promise). She took care of Sandy for me on the day of the move.

When March 3, 1997, came I was ready. Whenever I had moved before, I always had Dan there to help out; now I was on my own. And you know what? I did fine. I was certainly capable of making all of the arrangements, guiding the guys out the door of the old place, and leading them to my new home. They were so kind and helpful, and noticed right away the difference in the two places – especially the upbeat white walls of the townhouse. After everything was in place, I tipped them and took them to the nearby Luby's Cafeteria. I then went to Mother's to pick up Sandy, because I wanted my little dog to be there with me on my first night.

Sandy and I loved our new home. It didn't take long to get everything in place; I even had plenty of room for my antiques. I had already put in new carpet before I moved in, so there wasn't much left to do. I suppose I thought I was being quite the lesbian because I bought one of those rechargeable drills and used it to replace the knobs and handles in the kitchen. I know it sounds silly, but I was having fun taking care of my own place. That was a first for me.

T.J. called the next night to see how I was doing. I sat outside on my chair swing and chatted with her. I told her that I was happy and at ease with my new surroundings. I mentioned that I was outside looking at the moon from my little courtyard as I listened to my wind chimes. She said it made her happy to hear that I was so content.

Chapter 14

A woman had called me a few days before the move, telling me that she had read the *Observer* article and thought it was very brave of me to do it; she also said she would like to take me out to dinner. I will refer to her as "Jackie." She knew me through my PFLAG work, but I couldn't place her by name. The name was familiar, but I couldn't put a face to it. I told her that I was moving in a few days, so she asked me to call her after I got settled. I made the call, and we set a date. She picked me up, and took me to a nice, neighborhood restaurant. The food was great, and we had a good conversation. Afterward, Jackie drove me around my new neighborhood, showing me all the shops, grocery stores, etc. She brought me home, and later that night she called to say that she had enjoyed her time with me and would like to go out again. I said that would be fine with me.

The next morning she surprised me with a quick visit and some sweet rolls on her way to work. She apologized for not giving me a good-bye kiss the night before, so she gave me one before she left. And what a kiss! It was quite a turn on, and it felt completely natural to me. My first lesbian kiss. I still remember where I was standing.

Jackie was very brave to be my first girlfriend, not just due to the recent publicity, but because I was indeed a "late bloomer." One woman told me that she would be hesitant to date me, because she had been burned by a "new" lesbian who had come from a marriage to a man. She said sometimes those women decide to go back to their husbands or to men in general. I don't know how true that is, but it seemed to be a rather common presumption. I suppose time and experience would help that dilemma.

I believe Jackie would be called a "soft butch." Sorry about the classification. I mention that, because I began to understand the appeal of the "butch-femme" coupling. Guess it's also nice to not have both women hovering around the mirror applying make-up and hair spray. However, I did not feel locked into that preference. Jackie and I continued to date exclusively for almost three months, and the relationship became somewhat intimate. She was very attentive and around the Easter holiday, she brought me an Easter basket filled with my favorite diet treats and lottery scratch offs.

Since she was a member of several gay and lesbian organizations, we attended many parties together. I took her with me to the Second Annual Hope Awards, given by the Cathedral of Hope Church. I accepted their "Organization of the Year" award for PFLAG/Dallas. It was presented to me by Tim Seelig, long time director of the Turtle Creek Chorale.

I feel that the acceptance speech that I gave that night was the best speech I have ever given. It was not too lengthy, and I was very at ease and addressed the other recipients who were also at that 1992 protest of the National Affairs Briefing Meeting – people like John Thomas (winner of a "Special Award" that evening), Harryette Ehrhardt (She received the "Community Volunteer of the Year" award that night.), and Michael Piazza (minister of the Cathedral of Hope). I mentioned that protest earlier to you – the one attended by four of us PFLAG moms, the one where the police on horseback also attended.

I reminded the audience of the police, the candlelight vigil, the opposition waving their Bibles at us, etc. My speech ended with: "Never again will our national leaders speak that way about gays and lesbians in such a public place as our national conventions. Times have changed, and I would like to think PFLAG had a part in that, as did many of you sitting out there. We have all worked hard; we have a ways to go, but we will get there. Honors such as this one will certainly encourage our PFLAGers to hang in there. Thanks so much." I had written out my speech; but only took a few notes to the podium, and I was happy that I didn't have to look at those notes at all. Not sure I could do that today. Lory was in the audience, so I was especially happy that things had gone well.

I was also happy that Jackie was proud of me that night; we danced after the ceremony – my first lesbian dance. We continued dating, and even went on a vacation together. However, things did not work out between us. I felt she was a little too controlling, and I'm sure she thought I was too sensitive. I continued to date a few other women, but nothing serious or intimate developed. People told me that when I least expected it, someone special would come into my life. Bet you have heard that one before.

For some unexplained reason, the breakup with Jackie brought back my feelings for Lory. I was still having trouble getting over that woman. I asked her when that would happen, and she said, "When you find someone you want to spend the rest of your life with." Great. I couldn't believe that she continued to put up with me. She was very patient, and had gotten me involved in various committees so that I could meet people and become involved in the community.

I knew what I had to do, but it would be very painful for me. It was to force her to say that there was no hope for us, that she did not see me in that way. I knew deep down that was the case, but I needed to hear her say it. Earlier she had used the excuse of her girlfriend; they had broken up months ago. She was so afraid to hurt my feelings. She said after the pain she had in the past, she just couldn't say something that would hurt a person's feelings. She said that was just the way she was. I told her she would be doing me a service by being up front with me, that it would make it easier for me to move on.

So she finally said the words, that she did not see me in a romantic way. The words stung, but I thanked her for being honest with me; and I asked her how she had been able to hang in there with me. She said that a similar thing had happened to her many years ago. There was a woman who she was very attracted to, but the woman said she did not feel the same about her, but that she loved her as a friend. She may have made that up to make me feel better, but I don't think so. Lory said she wanted to remain my friend. I had always heard that lovers are easier to find than a lasting friend, that lovers come and go, but a good friend is forever. I teased her that maybe when we are really old and in our rocking chairs, we might get together, but she would have to be the butch one!

I talked with Brenda, my therapist, about this coming to terms with Lory. I mentioned that I wanted the sad feelings to be over, but she said they were necessary and good for me. She said that although the relationship between Lory and me had never been romantic or sexual, it was still a relationship and that what I felt was real. I said it was like finally finding that special person and losing her at the same time. She said that I must morn the loss. Great. I also mentioned to Brenda that I was a little frustrated trying to determine where I fit in the lesbian community and in the straight community. She said those things would just take time, not to rush anything and to stay true to myself.

Pat (18 months) and her mom, Martha Jo – 1944

Pat's old farm house in the 1950s. She is on the left. Farm was destroyed years later by a tornado.

Pat (age 17) with her dad & mom.
Wichita Falls, Tx 1959

Pat as a young bride at age 18.
Wichita Falls, TX 1961

Left to right: son, Brad, Pat, daughter, T.J., ex husband, Dan at
Brad's college graduation. Dallas, TX 1988

Pat as President of PFLAG/Dallas, marching in Gay Pride Parade.
Dallas, TX 1993

Pat, with former Texas Governor, Ann Richards; Dallas, TX 1995.
Pat's "before" photo - before losing 100 pounds.

Lory Masters, lesbian activist who was the catalyst for Pat's
"coming out." Dallas, Tx 1997

Photo by T.J. Friedel

Evie Kincaid, Pat's partner of 11 years, on a Nassau trip in 1999.

Pat, chatting with Hillary Clinton in Washington DC in 1998.

Christmas card photo of 2008. Evie, Scooter, Stormy, Daisy, and Pat.
Their home at the lake near Dallas, TX.

Pat Stone 2008
Five years since the gastric bypass surgery.

Chapter 15

I began to put my energy into the Late Bloomer group. We met a few times at my townhouse, then at various restaurants until we settled on a particular restaurant in the Oak Lawn area. At first the manager charged us a fee; but soon our numbers grew, and he dropped the charge. We brought in at least 20 women who bought dinner there on the second Tuesday of every month. The restaurant even had a private room for us. In fact, we continue meeting there still, for over eleven years now. I had some flyers and business cards printed that not only gave our meeting information, but included two lovely pink roses in full bloom. With the Late Bloomers, I began to see that I had found my *voice* again. It was just a quieter voice, but an important one.

From those early days, one of the women who still stands out in my mind is the woman who was a Mormon. She was devastated at the time, because she felt she would be excommunicated if her church found out about her new discovery. She came to our meetings several times, then moved away. She recently returned to Dallas with her partner of many years; they came to our meeting to thank us for the support they had received from us years ago. She said that was how she made it through her struggle with the church.

Many women come to our meetings for a while, get the support they need and move on; others continue to come regularly. They chat after our meetings; and often go out for coffee later, and perhaps go out to dance. Most are late bloomers like myself, but others are near our ages and have come out earlier. The women range from late 30s to 80s, with most being in their 40s, 50s and 60s; and they are from all backgrounds and religions. Now that many young people are coming out at the early age of 14, women in their 30s often feel they are "late bloomers." I feel that originally Late Bloomers was a spin off of PFLAG/Dallas, similar to another group called, "You Are Not Alone," a group for spouses who were married to gay or lesbian partners.

Late Bloomers is a safe place for women to come who need support, and it's a non threatening way to meet other women going through similar situations. I wish there had been a group like this when I came out. Many older women do not want to do the bar scene. We have helpful literature available; we have speakers most months, and we have parties and pot luck dinners. Many of us go to the local Blue Moon Dance.

Our speakers have ranged from therapists to long term lesbian couples. Lory has spoken to us, as well as Harryette Ehrhardt, Louise and Vivienne, therapist, Candy Marcum, etc. I have also asked some of our own members to tell us their story. We are not a formal organization – no 501(c)(3), no board meetings, no dues. Nor are we an advocacy group, because some of our members are closeted and fragile, while others are ready to enter additional lesbian organizations. Some of the women, especially when they first come in the door, feel very alone, fearing that they are the only ones in their situation.

Since I am not a trained therapist, I am careful to not give advise when I talk with a new person over the phone. I relate my story, offer them support, and tell them about our meetings. However, there was one case where I almost wanted to say, "Don't do this yet; don't leave your husband and child." The reason for that reaction was because as she was talking to me, I heard her husband in the background say a few words to her as he entered the room, and I heard her little girl telling her "good-night."

Also, the relationship with the woman she was seeing didn't sound very stable. But who am I to judge? I didn't know the whole situation, and the woman deserved to find her own way.

On the months that we decide to not have a speaker, we "chat amongst ourselves," which usually turns into one of our better meetings. It's fun to get them talking about their concerns and asking questions. Toward the end of that type of meeting, I often throw it out to "Hot Topics," inspired by "The View" TV show. Anything goes – politics, whatever.

Some of our more serious discussions involve child custody and often the loss of their best friend, their husband. However, I have seen many of the women remain friends with their ex-husbands. Some of the men are relieved to know that the problem within their marriage was not their fault. Less serious concerns center around dating - how to know if another woman wants to be a friend or a romantic partner, etc.

There are additional challenges such as financial concerns, religious concerns, explaining their situation to their children, getting comfortable with being lesbian and fitting in the lesbian community, losing some of their straight friends and family members, etc. A factor that is rather unique to us late bloomers is that we have elderly parents, who are often not familiar with the lesbian issue. Some women choose to not discuss their new found orientation with their parents, afraid it would be too upsetting for them. However, many of the parents do well with it after given some time. In fact, one mom often visits our meetings with her lesbian daughter. Another member told us that when she told her mom that she was gay, her mom said, "No, you're not." That was that!

On the positive side, the women have often found that missing piece of the puzzle to their lives; they have found themselves; and with that, a personal happiness and joy. Many find a partner and experience passion and romance for the first time; they get a second chance at life and find that "It's never too late." I have noticed that many of these women begin to see the world from a new perspective, becoming more tolerant of others who are different. They become more alive.

A common thread that I have seen in women who come out later in life is that they followed what they felt society wanted them to do – get married and raise children. Many, like myself, didn't know there were alternatives. I am rather thankful that I didn't know earlier, because I don't know how I would have handled the challenge of being gay and trying to raise my kids alone. However, I suppose I would have found a way.

I have seen many women who knew they had feelings for women while in college (and may had even acted on it); however, they felt it was just a phase that meant nothing of importance. They married and had a family; and years down the line, those feelings came back to them. Suppressed feeling can be a very dangerous thing; they can lead to much unhappiness - for the woman and later to the husband when she realizes her true orientation. I would think that with all the recent media coverage and discussion of gay and lesbian issues, there would be less coming out later in life. However, it's possible that some women will still suppress their feelings for various reasons – religious concerns, family influence, etc.

From what I have read recently, it seems that during mid life, husbands are more settled and happy with their life. However, wives have raised the kids and begin to look within themselves and question their inner happiness. That may lead some to see their suppressed orientation.

I would like to jump ahead for just a moment – to July of 1998. I invited Steve Blow from the *Dallas Morning News* to visit our Late Bloomer group and do a story on us if he felt it was worthy of media attention. I realize that I have mentioned Steve doing a few columns relating to gay issues, but most of his columns do not deal with that topic.

He covers a variety of subjects, from local community interests to humorous, folksy topics to very serious issues. It was my hope that if he did a story on us, it would reach women out there who were dealing with our situation. Steve did do a column on our group, and it was entitled: "Late Bloomers shake sexual foundations." It appeared in *The Dallas Morning News* on the front of the Metro section on July 22, 1998. He referred to our situation as a "mystery," and included quotes from various members of our organization. The article also mentioned my comment that most of the gay men I knew said that they realized they were gay all along. Steve added: "But women – herself included - buy into cultural images of romance as little girls and bury away any feelings in conflict with that."

I was happy with the column and I was relieved that Steve didn't seem to be unhappy about or judgmental of my new awareness. It was helpful that the column brought in several new Late Bloomers. I received eleven calls from women the first day that the article appeared.

It also brought an interesting phone call from a guy. One afternoon I came home to check my messages. This deep male voice said, "I know what you women need. You can call me at 1-800-BIG-DICK!

Chapter 16

Now back to 1997, and speaking of columns, I received from my mom a column in the mail plus a note. The column from the *Dallas Morning News* was titled "Life after loss is difficult soil to bloom in," by Dorothy Koch; it was published April 5, 1997. Ms Koch spoke of the sudden death of her husband, and she gave her readers important tips if they found themselves in difficult situations that year. She said: "Let time take its course as you prepare to start a new life. Remember that being happy is your choice to make every morning." She also recommended turning to faith and church, as well as to one's friends and family.

Mother, who rarely wrote about advice, sent along this note: "I couldn't help thinking of you when I read this article this morning. I want you to know that I will *always* be here for you & my prayers are with you *always*. I know this has not been all that easy for you. Don't think that I haven't seen the pain in your eyes at times. I hope you will find a church where you will be comfortable in & meet more friends and become active in helping others. Maybe you should give Dorothy Koch a call. I'll always love you, Mother" Like a lot of things, that note means even more to me now that it did at the time.

The spring of 1997, brought some interesting events. I and a young lesbian buddy ("Jenny") from PFLAG attended the Lesbian Conference in Houston, TX. I took a lesbian sex class, but it wasn't as exciting as it sounded – mainly dealt with safe sex and HIV. The highlight of the trip was meeting Col. Margaret Cammermeyer. You may remember that her life story was recounted in the TV movie, *Serving in Silence* – an adaptation from her book of the same name. It centered around the fact that she was kicked out of the military due to her orientation. She encouraged me to write a book about my experience; however, I decided it was too soon at that time.

Jenny and "Shannon," (another young PFLAG buddy), and myself drove to Austin, TX, for the "March on Austin"- supporting gay and lesbian rights. We marched with the PFLAG/Dallas chapter. It was such a fun trip, and I can't believe we made it in Jenny's old jeep. Guess I was making up for the loss of my teen years. They still laugh that I just sat on the grass before the march and made them put together our huge PFLAG banner.

That was nothing compared to the trip to the tattoo parlor in Dallas. I decided I wanted a butterfly tattoo on the left side of my upper chest! So Jenny and Shannon went with me and stayed outside the room, peeking through the glass. I had to be brave since they were watching me. It was painful at times, but the guy lifted up the needle often, which helped. It was a respectable and clean parlor. I thought a red butterfly would be nice – signifying my coming out of my cocoon and flying free.

Another fun spring event was the PFLAG "Ellen Watching Party" at my townhouse. It turned out that I came out just months before Ellen's character did on her TV sitcom. PFLAG chapters around the country were having "Ellen Watching Parties," especially for the segment where she told her family that she was gay. Shannon came that night as well as many PFLAG parents. It was fun and rewarding to be able to still participate in our local chapter.

The absolute most fun spring event of 1997, was the surprise presentation of a toaster oven to Lory Masters. I was having a PFLAG/Dallas pot luck party that day, May 4, 1997. John Selig and I thought it would be great to do a take off of the recent "Ellen Show" when Ellen's catalyst (Laura Dern's character) was presented with a toaster oven at the end of the "coming out" segment. We tried to copy it as best we could. We didn't want to do the gag in front of all the PFLAG parents; we only included a couple of Lory's friends and my pals, Jenny and Shannon (They took photos and a video).

When there was a lull in the party, I asked Lory to come upstairs to my office, that I wanted to show her something. All of a sudden, John handed me a clip board with several pieces of paper attached. John read the first line of: "Are you gay?" I replied, "Yes, I am." He said, "Then sign here." I rested the clip board on my desk and signed and dated the paper; John asked me to sign two more copies under the top page; he then stamped each page. Lory was speechless. John handed her the clip board and asked her to read it. She read: "Good For You. You're Gay." Question: "Are you gay?" Answer: "Yes, I am. And I was recruited by Lory Masters on July 11, 1996." When Lory got to that last part, she said, "Oh shit" and doubled over with laughter.

At that moment John uncovered a new toaster oven and handed it to her. She loved it and mentioned that it was about time she was getting one of those. What a perfect correlation – Ellen and her TV catalyst had not had a sexual relationship and neither had Lory and I, but toaster ovens were presented anyway! The presentation was fun. It served as another closure for me, but it also spoke volumes of a lasting friendship. Lory says even to this day that the award of the toaster oven was one of the highlights of her life.

I continued to date sporadically, but nothing developed. A couple of my gay guy friends even fixed me up with a blind date – not a good idea. Guess I was being rather picky. I enjoyed going out with my pals, Shannon and Jenny. We would dance at the lesbian bar, Sue Ellen's, go bowling, or just grab a bite to eat. I took lessons in golf, dance, and tennis – also bought a tent for camping. All those things were in preparation for being a good lesbian. I later realized that all lesbians do not like to do those things; I had a lot to learn.

The summer of 1997, brought me a much appreciated award – the Extra Mile Award. It is an award given to lesbians (and sometimes a gay man) who are cited for their support of the lesbian community. Again, I do not mention these things to brag; however, I am especially proud of this one, because it helped to disprove that comment made in the *Dallas Observer* by the lesbian who said: "And it's not like a bunch of politically active lesbians have offered her support." I did feel supported by many of the lesbian leaders of Dallas from the beginning, and I will always value that. I received notes, emails, and calls from numerous leaders, both lesbian and gay men.

For example, I will always be grateful for the supportive emails I received from Rev Carol West of the Cathedral of Hope back in January of 1997. Candy Marcum, a respected therapist and community activist, also sent me a nice email; she said that she was glad I did not come to her for therapy because then we could not be friends since I would be her client. I know that there were other gays and lesbians who were not supportive when I first came out, but I believe their numbers were few, and many reconsidered as time passed.

The winners of The Extra Mile Award were voted on by past recipients, an honor in itself. The award was given at an elegant ceremony at The Science Place in Dallas on June 28, 1997. My friend, John Selig, was my "date" for the evening. After I sat down from making my speech, an attractive butch lesbian hugged me and said, "You're such a sweet woman." I replied, "Not too sweet, I hope." Oops, I had to remember what my therapist had told me - to not change the values I had. Maybe sweet and sexy would be OK. By the way, I had lost more weight, and was at 159 – a long way down from that 265. I can't weigh much less than that or I appear rather gaunt; not sure why that is the case. Man, that was a 106 pound loss. It seemed easier to lose weight and maintain it when I was alone and on my own. Perhaps that was just my imagination. The Phen-Fen was the reason for most of the weight loss.

Chapter 17

The house in northeast Dallas finally closed on June 30, 1997. As it turned out, I felt it was a prequel to another major closing. Dan moved to a smaller house nearby, staying in the same neighborhood.

To me, one of the saddest things about the divorce was that Dan separated himself from my mom. I suppose that's not an unusual occurrence in a divorce; however Mother had always admired him so much, and she missed not hearing from him especially since they lived in the same part of town. I wrote him about her concerns, and he sent her a nice letter, trying to explain the situation. I won't quote from his letter, because it was private correspondence meant just for her; although I'm sure he knew she would share it with me.

He told her how much he had always admired her strength and grace. However, he added that at the time he needed to get past seeing me when he saw her. He said he would never forget her and hoped she would not forget him. That was back on April 30, 1997.

In August of 1997, things changed. Mother called Dan to touch base with him. She brought up my name later in the conversation; and he explained to her that to get through the situation, he no longer wanted to talk to me or see me. Mother was very distraught as she shared this information with me. She and I assumed it was just a short term solution for him.

To answer my earlier question at the beginning of the book as to whether I was being naïve to think Dan and I would remain friends and continue sharing holidays with our kids, the answer is "yes." I never counted on that reaction from Dan. It seemed that his big change in attitude came after our house sold, and he moved to his new place.

I will skip ahead and tell you now that this was not a temporary solution for Dan. Basically, this has been the situation for the last 12 years. Finally, I got tired of trying to reconnect with him. I felt I had handled things the best I could. My disappointment over his refusal to maintain any type of friendship with me vanished many years ago, but it took longer for me to adjust to his sometimes cool attitude toward me when I called his office to speak to Brad, or when I passed him in the hall or saw him in other places in Dallas.

I was left with trying to figure out where he was coming from. I finally decided it was his way of trying to close off the past. Perhaps during all of those times that I tried to explain things to him, he already understood those explanations; but he just did not want to be reminded of our past or what had happened. Things would have been so simple if he could have just been open and explained his position to me. Perhaps he didn't feel he owed me an explanation.

Something I want to make clear is that just because my ex husband did not react like I wanted (keep a family relationship of some kind) does not mean that I think he made a bad choice or the wrong choice. It simply caught me off guard; it was not what I expected, and I didn't understand. I later realized that I didn't have to understand. I should have stopped trying to explain my position to him, stopped trying to figure out *his* position. He made a decision that he seems happy with, a decision that works for him.

Also, it seems obvious to me that our kids (now grown adults in their 40s) do not have the need for us to remain a family. They are able to have good relationships with

Dan and me separately, and they have their own lives to lead. I decided to respect Dan's wishes, and we have both moved on. He has not remarried, but it appears that he is leading a full life, surrounded by many friends.

Chapter 18

And speaking of moving on...let's get *back* to 1997. Fall was approaching, and I had been out on my own for about six months. I spent a lot of time checking out job possibilities without success. I saw it was not easy for an older women without job skills, and a background in non-profits didn't seem to be helping me. I even wrote to Mayor Ron Kirk's office, asking to be considered as a participant if they decided to create an agency that would act as an outreach from the gay and lesbian community to the public sector. I had seen Mayor Kirk recently at an HRC function, and he smiled and said, "I've been reading about you coming out!" I was relieved that he did not seem bothered by that new information.

I continued the job search; however, I don't believe I saw how important a job might be at that time. I thought I had enough money safely invested in the stock market through a major financial institution. There goes that naïveté again.

Lory mentioned something about our both living alone and that it could get lonely sometimes. I told her that at that time I still liked living alone, and I still loved that townhouse. I told her that I only felt lonely sometimes when I came home after an activity and realized I did not have a relationship – no one to share my experiences with. The worst was that empty feeling after a party at my place, when all the guests had left. I mentioned that I did look forward to being in a relationship, but still living apart.

I briefly dated a woman who was very nice. She took me on a picnic in a lovely natural park area. She brought me flowers, had prepared food for us, even brought strawberries with melted chocolate. We spread every-thing out on a blanket; and after we ate, she taught me a little about backgammon. The chemistry just wasn't there, perhaps not for her either. She had come to PFLAG to meet me after the *Observer* article; she said I was cou-rageous to do the article, but she was afraid to get in-volved with me because I was so "out."

I began to wonder if I would ever meet "the" woman. Back then there were no respectable web sites to meet people as are available today. I asked Brenda during a therapy session why I could not meet someone that was fun like my buddies, but also a turn on to me romanti-cally. She told me to go home and make a list of all the characteristics that I would like in a woman. I came back with: (in no particular hierarchy)

1. Affectionate

2. Attractive – not too butch and not too femme

3. Humor – be fun

4. Have an "edge" – not bland, be strong

5. Sexual

6. Intelligent & interested in the gay & lesbian issues

7. Able to communicate feelings; good conversationalist

8. Happy with herself

9. Be "out" to family & hopefully to others

10. Sensitive – be a good listener

11. Interested in others – not just herself

12. Not a workaholic – be able to share her time with me

13. Trustworthy & honest – ethical

14. Can be laid back – does not have to be "on" all the time

15. Direct and up front

After bringing the list back to Brenda, she said for me to pick out the most important top five and work on those. I looked at the list again and marked: affectionate, attractive, sexual, an edge, honest/trustworthy, and I had to mark a sixth – humor. I suppose I had to be careful with that "edge" request; however, Brenda said she could see that I did not want a "milquetoast" woman.

I put dating on the back burner again and headed to Florida for the PFLAG National Convention; it was October of 1997. Going to the convention that year was very different for me. I attended as a Regional Director, and I went alone without Dan – both were firsts for me.

Two fun highlights were the winning of an "Ellen" TV script in the silent auction and marching outside the building with my sign that read: "Thanks Disney for Supporting My FAMILY!" The sign included my hand drawn Mickey Mouse silhouette.

I now have that script with its orange cover inside a glass enclosure, sitting on my coffee table. It's signed by the cast, and it's called "Roommates;" I think it's also referred to as "The Kiss." Disney had been catching a lot of flak due to being gay and lesbian supportive, so we at PFLAG wanted to show our support.

After returning from the convention, I prepared for my PFLAG/Dallas pot luck dinner party; which was October, 19, 1997, at my townhouse. I loved having parties out in that grassy communal area. My tables with the table cloths looked great out there. I was happy that Lory was going to attend as well as my mom and my son, Brad. He had really come along with accepting my situation; I was so happy about that. He used my video camera that afternoon and got some good shots of the party.

When Lory came to the door, she introduced me to someone she had brought with her. She said, "This is Evie." I tried to shake her hand, but I was holding something so I said that I would just give her a hug. She replied, "I'll take anything I can get." So that was Evie, who Lory had been with five years ago. They had been together for seven years, and I assumed they were trying to get back together. Evie and her recent partner of five years had broken up just a month earlier. Evie seemed very nice, was attractive, and we chatted as Lory and I showed her around my townhouse.

After seeing Evie, I knew why I had not been Lory's *type*. She was wearing snug jeans, boots, a shirt with the sleeves rolled up, and she had her salt and pepper hair cut short due to her work in landscaping. She owned her own business, E-Scapes, and I believe Lory had told me that she was 39 years old. I was hopeful that they would make a go of it this time around.

Many of my PFLAG friends came to the party, and Dave Gleason presented me with a framed plaque that read: "Our love and thanks go to Pat Stone for being an excellent spokesperson for the Dallas Chapter of Parents, Families and Friends of Lesbians and Gays." After dinner, I passed out large sugar cookies and tubes of frosting and other edible decorations. Everyone had a good time creating whimsical Halloween treats. They went well with the home made ice cream I had prepared – always the room mother.

A couple of days after that party, I found a note on my entrance floor; it had been dropped through my mail slot while I was out running errands. As I picked it up, I saw that the top of the note was personalized with the name "Evie Kincaid" in dark blue lettering. It read: "I enjoyed meeting you at the party on Sunday. Would really like to take you to dinner some evening. Give me a call (gave a number) – that's my daytime mobile or you can leave a message there also. Hope to hear from you. Evie" I was stunned by the note. I immediately called Lory and asked her what was this about. She laughed and said, "I guess she wants to take you out to dinner." I asked her why Evie would ask me out when she knew I was her friend. Lory said, "Hell, I don't know why she does half of the things she does." She said they were not back together, but had been seeing one another. Sounded like they had been rehashing the past.

I then called Evie and told her that I could not go out with her because Lory was my friend. Evie was working out at her health center at the time. She said that she respected my loyalty to my friend; but they had not been together in five years, and she hoped I would rethink my decision. I didn't know for certain what was going on with the two of them, but I didn't want to get involved. It was important to me to keep Lory as my friend, so I didn't want to intrude (even though I did find Evie attractive).

October 1997, came to a close with my having the opportunity to meet Cecile Richards, daughter of former Texas Governor, Ann Richards. At that time she was director of the Texas Freedom Network, an organization in opposition to the "Religious Right's" intrusion into politics. Cecile flew into Dallas to speak to PFLAG/Dallas. I picked her up from the airport and we joined John Selig and his son at a restaurant near the meeting location. She was so laid back, humorous, and gracious; and she did such a good job as she spoke to our PFLAGers. On the way back to the airport, we talked a little about our private lives, about my recent divorce and the fact that her parents had divorced when she was a child. She was a very warm person.

I believe that November 8, 1997, was one of the most significant dates for gay and lesbian rights at that time. It was the date of HRC's National Black Tie Dinner in Washington, D.C., and it was the first time a sitting President had addressed a gay and lesbian group. HRC was the largest gay and lesbian organization in the nation. The President who achieved that recognition was President Bill Clinton. I was thrilled that I was able to attend such an historic event, and who better to share such an evening with than Louise and Vivienne, and Lory. All three were near my table. When President Clinton walked out on stage, I was surprised at what a large man he was – even though I had heard that fact many times. The comment that he made that I most remember was that gay rights are civil rights, and they should be law.

After he spoke he came down into the crowd. I passed by Lory's table on my way to get closer to Clinton. I stopped and saw she was in tears. I gave her a hug and told her that she had seen many changes in her life, but I bet she never thought she would see this. She said, "Never." We hugged, and I gave her a kiss on the cheek. I walked on and was able to shake President Clinton's hand.

Louise was near me in the crowd and had shook his hand also. She said to me, "I'm so glad you were able to be here for this." I took Louise to Lory's table and they hugged and cried. I told them I wanted to take a photo of the two of them, and I was able to get someone to take one of all three of us. As we all sat back down for the rest of the program, I thought about all the work those two women had done for the community, and how they had made it easier for me (and many others) to come out years later.

The HRC program continued after President Clinton made his exit. Ellen DeGeneres did a very nice (what seemed to be an "off the cuff") talk with the audience, explaining that she had been hesitant to come out in the press. She had dodged the question, thinking it was her personal business. However, after seeing all the discrimination and learning of the suicide statistics concerning gay teens, she had changed her mind. She added, "If telling the truth is an activist, then I'm an activist."

I was privileged to talk to the actress, Judith Light, who was at the dinner that night. I knew she had spoken out for gay and lesbian rights many times, but I couldn't believe how approachable and friendly she was. I told her my story, and she seemed very interested. I asked if I could snap her picture, and she said to wait; she gave my camera to her friend and asked him to take our picture together. What a nice gesture. What a wonderful evening.

Chapter 19

After returning to Dallas, I began to question my decision regarding Evie. I certainly did not want to ruin my friendship with Lory. I would wait until after our local Black Tie Dinner on November 22, and see how they were doing at that time. Perhaps they would be at the dinner together. I had already confided in my friends Shannon and Jenny, and they thought by the tone of my voice that I was going to call Evie back. Jenny asked me if part of my interest in her was that she had been with Lory. I was shocked by that question; for some reason, the fact that she had been with Lory was a negative to me. I think I saw it as causing a wedge between Lory and myself.

Well, things fell into place for me. After a PFLAG meeting, a gay guy friend told me that he had seen Lory with a cute, young, butch woman and that they were dating. So I called Lory to see if she minded my going out to dinner with Evie. She said that was fine with her, that they were not getting back together. I mentioned that Evie might be too butch for me. She said no, that Evie could appear many different ways, that she could go out to elegant places with her tiny ear rings, a little make up, and silk slacks or she could be very butch.

I had to think of a reason to call Evie, a reason besides saying I would go out with her. When I called she was about to close on a small house she had recently bought. I told her that I was thinking of writing a book (true, but it took me another eleven years to do it), and I might want to refer to her in connection with Lory. Would she mind if I used her real first name? She said that would be OK with her. I then told her that I had talked to Lory, and she did not mind if I went out with her. Gee, I was still back in junior high. She laughed and said she was glad I had changed my mind. We made a date for Tuesday, November 18th, 1997.

When I greeted Evie on my door step that evening, I was stunned. She was a "cool" looking woman; her hair had grown out from that buzz cut, and she was wearing black slacks with a lovely silver (matched her hair) jacket. She also had on those tiny ear rings that Lory mentioned. I told her she looked cute (can't believe I wasn't able to come up with something better than that), and she said, "It wasn't easy." She had been working outside a lot that day, and she said it took her hours to clean up. When I hear the song, "Something About the Way You Look Tonight" by Elton John, I always think of seeing her that night on my porch. You know, I had never paid much attention to love songs until that time in my life.

We had a nice, quiet dinner that evening, as we shared many stories from our past. Evie carried a lot of guilt concerning her son, John. I told her that I felt it was undeserved guilt. He was just a baby when she realized she was lesbian; she was in her early twenties at that time. When she and her husband divorced, Evie lost custody of John. It wasn't always easy back then for a lesbian to win custody of her child.

Shortly after that, she became involved in drugs, and her parents sent her to rehab at Hazelden, an outstanding center in Minnesota. I already knew from talking to Lory that Evie had a drug problem about 20 years earlier. She had done well at Hazelden; she completed the program and continued to live there for another 2 years after getting a job. Evie returned there years later to give a speech regarding her recovery and her time spent at Hazelden.

Man, I had wished for a woman with an edge – a slight edge. I hoped Evie did not have too sharp of an edge for me.

I asked her about the note she had dropped in my mail slot, and she said she was so happy I didn't see her as she ran up to my door. She and her truck were very muddy from work, and it was even raining at the time. Evidentially, leaving me that note was a little forward for her. She had talked to one of her favorite clients, an older straight women who was very proper and mannerly. She told the women about meeting me and that she wanted to go out with me, but wasn't sure how to handle it. Her client said, " Evie, it's always proper to send a lady a thank you note regarding her party."

After dinner, Evie brought me home and came in for a minute to see Sandy. She even left my front door wide open the whole time! She petted Sandy and gave her a kiss on the head and told me good night and that she had a good time. I left her a message that night that I had lost a button from my sweater that evening (true), and asked if she would look for it in her car. She later called me back to say she had not found it. I asked her if she wanted to go out again, and she said she definitely did want to go out, perhaps the next week. I asked her about her departing behavior, and she said she did not want to come on too strong and wanted to be respectful.

We planned our second date for Wednesday, November 26th – the day before Thanksgiving. In the meantime, we saw each other at the Dallas Black Tie Dinner on Saturday, November 22. Evie had previously committed to go with her recent ex (not Lory), and I was going with my buddy, Shannon. I originally thought that Shannon would be wearing a red cummerbund, so I bought a sexy red dress with silver beading and sequins. Of course, most people wear black or white to a Black Tie affair – oh, well. Shannon and I went shopping at the tux rental store, and she decided on a more traditional tux and black cummerbund. We had such fun in that place.

T.J. and her partner came to Dallas for the dinner, mainly to meet Evie and to hear Maya Angelou speak. Elizabeth Birch gave an enthusiastic speech as always, and Ms Angelou's presentation was very dramatic and sensitive. Who would not love that voice? During a break in the festivities, T.J. was able to meet Evie and say a few words to her. She told me later she was very impressed with her. Evie later mentioned that when we were all dancing after the dinner, her ex said, "That woman in the red dress is looking at you." I came very close to asking Evie to dance, but decided that might be rude. Because of that evening, one of Evie's favorite songs became, "Lady in Red."

I was very excited about our second date. I wasn't about to let Sandy steal the show this time; in fact, I dropped her off at Mother's to spend the night (Mother owned Sandy's sister, Gigi). I chose the restaurant, Jaxx Cafe, which was not far from my townhouse. It was one of those intimate places with tablecloths (I guess I have a thing about tablecloths). After our lovely meal, we came home, sat on my couch and watched "Ellen" together. I could not believe the subject of that particular episode. Ellen and her girlfriend were going to have sex for the first time, and Ellen (being a new lesbian) was worried that she would not know what to do. I had little experience in that area and the same thing was going through my head. Evie had been "out" for almost 20 years and had much, much more experience.

Evie was sitting to my left, and I was sitting next to the arm of the couch; her glass of water was on the table next to me. During the TV show, she occasionally reached across me to get her water. She made the first move by casually putting her hand on my knee. After the show was over, she started reaching for her water, and I said, "If you reach across me one more time..." I was about to finish that sentence with "I am going to kiss you." However, she beat me to the punch and gave me a wonderful kiss.

It became obvious that I didn't want things to end there. Evie asked, "Are you sure about this?" I said, "Yes." Not knowing what to do was far from my mind. As things began to progress, I said, "I guess this is when I should ask if you have been tested for AIDS? She laughed and said, "Yes I have, but you sure waited to the last minute to ask." On our first date, as I shared with her my coming out story, I also told her about my being tested for AIDS after my divorce. I said there was not a chance I had it unless it came from dental work; but I knew women would want to know since I had been with a man. Of course, my test was negative.

Evie was fantastic that night, and she later told me that she would have never known that I was an inexperienced lesbian. I took that as a nice compliment. She was surprised that I was ready to move along that fast on the second date. I told her that I was 54 years old, that I didn't have time to play all the games. She didn't leave my townhouse until around 4 am the next morning; in fact, the Thursday morning paper was already on my lawn. I had to get up in a few hours and put my turkey in the oven! My buddies, Shannon and Jenny would be sharing Thanksgiving dinner with me. I wondered if they would see the smile on my face.

Yes, they did see that coy smile, and they also noticed the hickey on my neck; I wore it as a badge of honor – my first hickey. They were very happy for me and continually teased me about my night of passion. We three had a great time that day. My turkey turned out perfectly, and Shannon did the honor of carving it. I had also made my mom's famous sweet potato casserole with the brown sugar, corn flakes, and pecan topping – as well as a broccoli casserole, mashed potatoes, and mini pecan pies.

Before we sat down to eat, I read from a passage that I had framed in 1983; it was an alternative definition of a family that was always read to friends at the Thanksgiving celebration at "Brushyland." It came from a book by Jane Howard called *Families*. It read:

A Family Is:

"a bunch of people who rush to each other's side in an emergency.
made up of people who observe rituals (birthdays, Thanksgiving, Christmas) together.
someone you spend time with even if it's not always fun.
people who don't have to be nice to each other.
a group of people with a common history strong enough to imply a common future.

Thus, the definition of the family has been extended to include all those people you care about and share experiences with, whether you are related to them by birth or by nothing more biologically binding than friendship."

Evie and I continued to date exclusively. She took me shopping and bought a pair of western boots for me. We also tried to go to a movie, but we had to leave because we couldn't sit that close to each other without getting romantic ideas. One particular evening I stayed the night at her house, and during an intimate moment, I yelled, "Evie, there's a fire!" She had not noticed, but the candle next to the bed had caught the pillowcase on fire. She quickly threw a glass of water on it and pounded out the flames. We learned to never put a candle near the bed!

There was a moment at my townhouse that I looked at her and said, "We're in trouble, aren't we?" She said, "Yes." We meant that the relationship was taking a very serious turn. It was no longer just about romance and intimacy. I had not planned on a serious, committed relationship at this point. I had just come out of a 35 year relationship. Evie was chatting to me, and I heard something within her words that sounded like "I love you." I asked her to repeat that, and she said, "I love you." I said that I also loved her. However, I told her that I was not ready for us to move in together, because I wanted to continue the romantic dating phase. I loved having her pick me up and take me out to dinner, etc. I also loved living alone, as long as I had someone special in my life.

Evie continued to stay at my place most of the time. What bad timing that she had just bought a house before we became involved. It was obvious that she was getting tired of dragging her things back and forth between our houses. Her dog, Stash, (a Schnauzer) came to live with Sandy. They got along OK, but it appeared that Sandy felt rather intruded upon. You see, Sandy never felt she was a dog; so she didn't know what to make of that black and gray animal following her around. Soon, the four of us became a happy blended family.

Chapter 20

I received an exciting call from one of the producers of the TV show "20-20;" he had gotten my name and number from National PFLAG. He was interviewing women who had come out later in life for a segment of the show. We talked at length, but I told him that I knew my ex husband would not participate. I felt that was a major reason I was not chosen – plus also having a lesbian daughter sometimes complicates the issue. However, when I watched the finished product on December 4, 1997, on "20-20," I saw that they did fine without me. The segment was called, "Coming Out in Midlife," and the couples did a great job. The presentation dealt with women coming out later in life, and their husbands spoke of the impact it had on their lives. All husbands were stunned with their wives new discovery. Several of the couples had been married for 17 to 25 years and had children.

One husband remarked that he didn't understand how his wife could have been gay because she responded to him sexually, that their sex life had been good. It was pointed out that sex is just one part of being a lesbian; emotional attachments and who a person could be intimate with was also important.

Another husband, who was in tears, pointed out that a big problem for him was the fact that he still loved his wife very much, and he wanted her to be happy; but that would mean the end of the relationship he had with her.

A wife told viewers that a person can't be "turned" gay; she just realizes she is; she discovers who she is.

She can't close the door once it is opened. A therapist pointed out that mid life seems to be a trigger. At that time women want to be themselves. Before that time, it was too threatening to be gay; it threatened their dreams of marriage and family. Some women do not let these feelings out; many try to bury their new found discovery.

A woman said the word "lesbian" was not a fit for her when she thought of her marriage, even though she knew she did not feel the passion and desire that other women spoke about. As years passed, she saw the word was a fit after all. Often the wives were the most surprised by their discovery. They knew something was wrong, and most felt their husbands were OK – so something must be wrong with them, but what? "20-20" described this occurrence as a change of heart from a voice within – a mid course correction in their sexual identity.

Another woman lamented that she would be destroying her family, and that she couldn't change the hurt. She was asked why she couldn't stay married for the sake of the kids. She replied that she had become suicidal, that she had tried very hard to be happy; but she just couldn't keep doing that.

A teenaged son of one of the couples said at first he worried about his friends finding out, and he had been angry with his mom; but now he was "cool" with it, and he added "you can't dislike a person for who she loves."

Chapter 21

The 1997 Christmas holiday was approaching; but since the relationship between Evie and me was only a month old, we decided against celebrating with each others family that year. It seemed a little soon for that. By the way, we marked our relationship starting on that second date, November 26, 1997.

Evie did take me by her parents home; they had a lovely place in the prestigious Park Cities area of Dallas. I met her mom, and I really liked her and knew right away that we would get along well. I suppose only being one and a half years apart in age helped! She had Evie when she was about 17.

Yes, there was a 15 year age difference between Evie and me. People told us that we didn't look that far apart, and Lory said that Evie was an "old soul," so maybe the age difference would not be a big deal. At least we agreed on a few musical selections, one in particular – "Unchained Melody" by the Righteous Brothers. It quickly became "our song." I teased Evie, telling her to keep letting her hair go silver and to continue working out in the sun – then perhaps we would always look near the same age. Of course, I knew the face lift helped me out a little.

She and I visited Jessica near the holidays. They seemed to connect with one another right away. Jessica wasn't feeling very well and said she was ready to go. (However she managed to live another six months and saw her son married.) We talked to her about my working with Evie, doing her invoices, etc. Jessica said she would advise against it, that it could harm our relationship (and she was right). The three of us had a lovely talk, and after Evie and I gave her a hug good-bye, she said to Evie "take care of her." Evie replied, "I will try."

Jessica had never been able to visit my townhouse after I had moved in, so I made a video for her, showing the placement of my furniture; but mainly showing her the lovely wall paper that she had picked out for me. I also told her "good-bye" in the video and mentioned how much her friendship had meant to me. I still think of her often.

I missed seeing Lory. Occasionally she and her new partner and Evie and I would go out to dinner; however, Lory's schedule was always so busy that those evenings were few in number. She called me one afternoon, something about my Christmas gifts from her. I told her that I still needed her in my life, and she said she would always be there for me. She said she loved both me and Evie and didn't want any hearts to be broken. I said I knew that I could get hurt; Lory replied that Evie could also.

T.J. and her family came to Dallas to share an early Christmas with me, as well as with her dad. She now had to spend just a few days with me and then go to Dan's for a few days. It worked out fine. T.J. and her family plus Brad and myself went to Mema's and Sam's to have dinner and open presents. Mother played her harmonica for us; she has always been quite the harmonica player. She learned as a kid from her brothers and played by ear. She was also very talented at the piano and the organ.

Evie took me to the Melrose, an old, exquisite hotel in Dallas, to celebrate our own private Christmas. We had a very romantic evening. She had even arranged for a woman violinist to play for me, and she ordered a very fancy breakfast to be sent to the room the next morning.

A couple of days later on December 22, we joined a few of my friends at a nice restaurant to celebrate my

55th birthday. Guests included: my son, Brad, Lory and her daughter, Lory's partner, John Selig and his son, John's partner, Shannon and Jenny. After dinner we went to my townhouse, where Evie presented me with a very special birthday cake.

When Christmas Day rolled around, T.J. and family had returned to their home to have Christmas there. So back to the Chinese restaurant for Brad and me; this time we added Shannon and Jenny, and Mema. We had a great time, and then went to Mema's house to hear her play Christmas carols on her piano. My friends gathered around her and sang along - a lovely moment.

I had a very nice holiday, which marked a little over a year since I came out. Things had settled down since last year, since Christmas of 1996. I considered myself very lucky to have so many supportive people in my life. It could have ended up quiet differently.

As I packed away my decorations, I addressed the note from last year, which said: "Where will I be, who will I be with (if anyone), and what will be my mood when I unpack these things next Christmas?"

It was interesting because I unpacked those decorations even before Thanksgiving – on November 14, 1997 – due to the fact that T.J. came to Dallas for the Black Tie Dinner and an early Christmas celebration. On that day in November I wrote about my lovely townhouse in north Dallas, and that my mood was good – that I did have some down times, but not often. I mentioned that I was trying to find my niche, but I had no regrets. I added that I was with no one at that time, but that I had talked to Evie Kincaid that day, and that we would go out the following Tuesday.

I added to that note before I put away the box of decorations: "Evie is here with me. We are celebrating being together for five weeks tonight! I love her very much. We seem well-matched. We are not living together, but are only dating each other. I'm very happy."

Chapter 22

So this brings to a close the specific events that were very important to me during the two years (1996-1997) that encompassed my startling new awareness. Like many issues, "coming out" is a process that continues through out ones' life. As you saw, during those two years, the gay issue was very prominent in my every day experiences.

At this time, I would like to continue my conversation with you – touching upon a few areas of interest that occurred during the latter 10 years of my life. However, I will not address this section in such chronological detail as before. The gay and lesbian issue will still be part of my life, but not the main focus. I want to share with you my life with Evie, perhaps to show that our life is very much like the average persons' out there – gay or straight. We have had our ups and downs, our happy moments and our tragedies.

In early 1998, Evie sold her house (at a nice profit) and moved in with me. I had mixed feelings about it, because I did not want our romantic life to suffer; however, I knew our relationship was ready for the next step.

Evie and I were opposites in many ways, so we had to become accustomed to those differences. You know how it is when you are dating someone and everything they do seems attractive? And then later it is no longer that appealing? That happened to me in regard to her smoking. I had always been such an anti-smoking person, but Evie only smoked occasionally when we first met. Also, I hate to admit it, but I thought she looked rather "cool" when she smoked – at first. Remember, I was still a teenager at that time and was taken with her "edge."

At my townhouse I would go outside in the cold, wrapped in a blanket, just to sit with her as she smoked. But then she began to smoke more and more; she began to smoke inside; she began to smell like cigarettes; I began to resent being near the smoke; she often left me at parties and other functions so that she could go outside and smoke. I hated the whole thing. Evie tried to quit by using the nicotine gum, but continued smoking and also chewing the gum. After a serious bronchial infection, she put the cigarettes down and has never returned to them. That made me very proud of her, because I know that is supposed to be one of the hardest addictions to break.

I am sure Evie discovered things about me that she was not crazy about also. I can name two right off the top of my head. She did not find some of my "straight woman" shirts attractive – you know, the ones made from T- shirt material with all the decorative brads and studs on the front. Also, she was not fond of my holiday yard art – the wooden Santa, the wooden Thanksgiving turkey and the wooden Easter bunnies. All those items went into a garage sale.

From a more serious point of view, I thought Evie tended to have a slight problem with mood swings (one of her former girlfriends referred to them as her "intensity"). And I did not help the situation, because I let my moods be affected by hers. If she snapped at me, I would not let it pass, but would often accelerate the situation. I believe that was due to my never being able to "talk back" when I was a kid. Also, perhaps this was what my therapist meant when she said that when I got into a relationship with a woman, it would be very intense. I kept working on ways to counter without accelerating.

If Evie became a little bossy at times, I felt I had to show her that I could stand up for myself. My friend, John Selig, has said many times that people when they first meet me think I am very nice and calm and perhaps easy to run over. He adds that when I am confronted, they see a different side than they thought was there. I suppose that's OK as long as I don't let it get out of hand and can be respectful of an opposing view.

I had a hard time realizing that if Evie and I argued, it wouldn't be the end of the relationship. Nor did it mean that she no longer loved me. We got along so well most of the time; so when we did argue, I tended to feel that things were ruined. It was the "other shoe dropping" from my childhood. Only time took care of those insecurities.

As I mentioned earlier, I tried working for Evie, but that didn't work out very well. Her landscape business seemed to be mostly a one woman operation – plus the guys who did the labor for her. Also, as Jessica had predicted, it was beginning to wear on our relationship.

However, I did get a very nice job with a client of Evie's; in fact, I worked for that company for several years. It involved general office work – from answering the phone, handling rebates, booking trips, etc. My title was "Senior Executive Assistant." It was there that I met a very fun and interesting young man that has remained my friend to this day. We still make time for occasional lunches and phone calls. I will call him "Marcellos."

We clicked from the first time we met. He dubbed me "The Office Mom." I suppose I could have been his mom since he was only one year older than my daughter. We had such fun at work. He even learned to dodge my occasional rubber band shots. He still reminds me that "the Office Mom is honest to a fault." That is a reference to the time I told my boss that people had said that about me. I shared that quote with him because he was about to give me the key to open the office in the mornings. My boss was not that impressed; he just replied, "As you should be."

Marcellos still laughs about the time I called him into the copy room for a "conference." I had gained some weight and had been dieting (again), and I had mentioned that I wanted to get to my goal weight before a business cruise that Evie and I would be attending. Marcellos teased me a couple of times that I would be looking good in my bikini by the deadline for the trip. I let him know that a woman of a certain age and size did not like hearing herself and the word "bikini" in the same sentence. He immediately apologized. He later referred to that conversation as involving the "b" word. He respected me for making him aware of something he had not realized.

On the flip side, Marcellos certainly made me aware of something also. He is African American, and I only add that because of the following incident. We were chatting one morning before work as we sat at our desks. He casually mentioned something about having some new stereo equipment in the trunk of his car the night before. He off-handedly said it was OK because he had the receipt with it in case he was stopped by the police. It began to sink in what he meant. Just because he was black, a police officer might very well assume it was stolen property.

Being white, I had never had such a thought concerning myself; it would never have crossed my mind. How unfair, to say the least. I talked to him about this, and he added that there were sections of Dallas that he knew never to go especially at night. It was sad to me that these things were part of Marcellos' daily life.

Chapter 23

There were a few years after Evie and I were first together that we were able to do a little traveling; most was spent visiting my daughter and her family. In fact, on our first trip there, Evie and I went on a romantic canoe trip. Out in the middle of the lake, we professed our love with a few unscripted words and exchanged rings. We did not take the route of many of our friends; we never had a commitment ceremony. Evie said they were the "kiss of death" for her, that she had done them several times in the past; and the relationships never lasted. I guess it would have been fun to have had one – an excuse for a party, something nice to do as a couple. However, I never pushed it, and we have now been together for 11 years – as of November 26, 2008. This is Evie's longest relationship. We feel that we have a strong inner bond that will keep us together through whatever we must face – not that there haven't already been challenges.

One of our earliest trips was to a rustic, getaway cabin in Oklahoma. It was a very romantic time for us – cooking smores in our fireplace, taking walks in the woods, and staying in bed for hours. During one of our days there, we drove to a small nearby store for snacks. Inside the store, I casually reached out to touch Evie's arm. She quickly moved away and told me not to do that; she whispered that we must be careful. She later reminded me that we were in a country area where it could be dangerous if some wacko knew we were a couple. I will never forget that moment. Here I had found someone I wanted to be affectionate with, but I had to be very careful about even a casual touch. This was new territory for me.

Evie and I have always loved to go to the State Fair of Texas in Dallas. We still visit there several times each fall. We love trying the latest deep fried treats, and of course, the Fletcher's corny dogs are the very best. My favorite desserts are the warm, delicious fudge, the cinnamon rolls, and funnel cakes. Evie loves the Tornado Taters. The midway lures her to try her luck at knocking the rubber chicken (or frog) into a tub by using a mallet. One of our favorite spots is the calm lagoon area, where we still love riding the swan paddleboats at sunset.

On September 25, 1998, as we sat relaxing by the edge of the lagoon, I handed her the following note: "Merry Christmas - a little early. How about a day trip to Washington, D.C. on Tuesday, October 6, 1998? Let's go to the home of Senator Edward Kennedy and chat with First Lady Hillary Rodham Clinton and Tipper Gore. We leave Dallas at 10:30 am and return at 10:22 pm. I love you, Pat"

Evie was very excited about the trip. She couldn't believe I had it all planned. I had received the invitation through The Women's Leadership Forum of the Democratic National Committee. The two women (Hillary and Tipper) were being honored at the home of Senator Kennedy and his wife, Victoria Reggie Kennedy. It was a rather small gathering so we were able to see the participants up close and personal. Evie and I felt very honored to be in the Kennedy's home, and we loved walking through their house and seeing many of their family photos. Hillary gave a very warm and courageous speech that night; as you may remember, that period of time was not easy for her. I was also quite impressed with Victoria; she had a real warmth and grace about her.

I have a great photo that was taken as I was talking with Hillary Clinton. I also took some shots and sent a framed one to Victoria along with a thank you note; the photo was of her and Hillary. I received a lovely personal note from her. That trip was short, but quite an experience.

Evie and I were able to spend more time on a trip to New York the next year. I booked a couple of plays – one on Broadway (*Hairspray*) and an off Broadway play (*Love, Janis*). We did some of the typical tourist things; but our friend, Paul, who lived in New York at that time, showed us some of the more off the beaten track parts of New York City. We had such a fun and relaxing time. Evie loved just walking the streets – even getting caught in a wind storm was exhilarating.

The only sad part of the trip was our visit to Ground Zero, the site of the 9-11 tragedy. Like everyone, Evie and I remembered where we were when that terrible event occurred. I was in the kitchen, watching my little TV as I loaded the dish washer; Evie was about to back her truck out of our garage as she was leaving for work. I saw what was happening and ran to tell her before she left. She immediately got out of her truck – leaving the engine running and the truck door open. We quickly turned on the den TV and sat there the rest of the day, trying to make sense of what had happened.

One of our more unique trips was a visit to Las Vegas, celebrating Evie's son's 21st birthday. Actually the idea came from Evie's ex husband, "Frank." He knew Evie would want to be part of John's special birthday; so he invited her, myself, and Evie's brother to go along. He even got us complimentary rooms and took us all out for a very expensive dinner. Now, that's a modern family gathering! Evie even helped Frank shop for a gift for his girlfriend.

Compared to some of our friends, we certainly were not world travelers, but we managed a few additional trips – to Atlanta (loved seeing the original works of Norman Rockwell), Santa Fe, a cruise, Shreveport, etc. Unfortunately, most of our travel has been curtailed for several years now. Remember the fall of the stock market, especially the tech stocks in 2000? My new financial adviser invested my funds in basically all tech stocks, and I took a real beating – losing most of the money that I thought was safely invested. I should have known better; in fact, I later learned that a person in her latter 50s should have had a more conservative portfolio. However, most people seemed to think back then that a way to make big money was to heavily invest in those tech stocks.

To make matters worse, I had just recently quit my job in order to spend more time with my mom. I thought that she might be having some memory problems – nothing serious, but I wanted to keep a check on her. Evie decided to sell her landscape company in order to go to work for a major "big box" company that would give her some needed benefits. She became a manager in their landscape division. Paying the large premiums on our insurance policies had become very difficult for us. Unlike married couples, we did not have spousal coverage. However, there have been some positive changes in that area with many companies over the last few years.

One of the upsides of my being home at that time was that it made it easier for Evie and me to bring into our family a beautiful grey and white Schnauzer puppy, named Daisy. Now we had "yours, mine, and ours." Stash and Sandy were getting older, and we thought they might like a little sister. Daisy did spice things up a bit; sometimes she was a little rough with Stash, and Sandy sort of looked down her nose at this rowdy newcomer. However, they soon learned to get along, and our family became complete.

I came home one afternoon many months later after running errands, and found Sandy lying on her side in the court yard under a tree; her beautiful red hair blowing softly in the breeze. She had gone out the doggy door, and I hoped died peacefully. I immediately called Evie in tears, and she rushed home, wrapped her in a blanket and we took her to the vet. We said it was just like Sandy – to die with dignity and to not bother anyone. The vet said it was kidney failure, and there was nothing we could have done.

Within the year, Stash had a stroke, and Evie had to make the painful decision to put her down. We will always remember Stash as she lay on the rug in Evie's office as Evie cradled her; little Daisy slowly walked over to Stash and laid her head on her. She sensed Stash was seriously ill. We knew Sandy and Stash were getting old, but we sure weren't ready to lose them.

Later Daisy seemed to need a playmate, so we brought home another Schnauzer puppy that we named "Stormy;" she turned out to be a lovely salt and pepper combination. She and Daisy became great pals and looked so cute together – a perfect "twosome." Within a few months, Evie brought home a dog that she had rescued at work. At first, I was not happy about that at all; I didn't think we needed three dogs, but I soon grew to love little Scooter. She was not a pretty dog, but became cute in her own way. She appeared to be part Dachshund, part Miniature Pinscher, part whatever; she had large ears and a slick black and brown coat. When Evie found her, she was badly scraped on her back and on one leg. Scooter loved Evie and still does; the feeling is certainly mutual.

So our three dogs – Daisy, Stormy, and Scooter started out with us at the townhouse and have remained with us to this day. Daisy is now ten years old (with beautiful long lashes), and she's the apple of my eye. Stormy and Scooter are six years old and love to chase one another through out our house. Evie and I love watching the interaction among the three of them. They bring us such joy, and we have had them on our Christmas cards all of their lives. Perhaps this is more than you wanted to know about our "babies."

Chapter 24

In addition to having more time to spend with my mom (and with my new pup, Daisy), I was also able to get involved again with a few PFLAG related issues. As part of the National Coming Out project, I had the honor of meeting and working with Betty DeGeneres (Ellen's mom). Nancy McDonald, President of National PFLAG, also came to Dallas for the event. Betty and I hung out for a while during that day, and I enjoyed seeing her in action as she handled the press over the phone. She was very smooth and effective. At that time, she was a spokesperson for HRC. The next day she, Nancy, John Selig, and I did an interview on KERA radio.

Evie and I were chaperons at a "Gay Prom" that was sponsored by Dallas/PFLAG. We will always remember the protesters in front of the building with their hateful signs. The kids inside did not let the signs spoil their fun; however, a young girl said initially she was afraid to come in the building due to the protesters. We had a uniformed police woman there, as well as several PFLAG dads and moms. There were no problems.

I was part of a large demonstration against one of our local TV stations that was about to air a proposed program of Dr. Laura Schlessinger. She had suddenly become quite outspoken about gays and lesbians – referring to them as "deviants and "biological errors" – as mentioned in the *Dallas Voice* on April 21, 2000. My good friend, John Selig, was one of the leaders of this "StopDrLaura. com" online campaign to stop her because of her anti-gay rhetoric. (John is still the activist; in fact, you can google his name and find his pod cast interviews; I am even included.)

My protest sign read: "Dr. Laura, What changed your mind since we spoke 5 years ago?" This was in reference to a message I had left for her in 1995, asking her opinion of "gay marriage." She had actually called me back. I wanted her opinion on that issue since she often spoke against couples "shacking up." At that time, she told me that she was in favor of same sex marriage, but it would have to be called something beside "marriage." Unfortunately, she may have been right about that. Even today many Americans are in favor of legal rights for gays and lesbians, but they are not ready for "marriage" to include same sex couples. I suppose I could live with that, as long as there are alternative provisions such as civil unions containing the same rights. However, it appears that at this time the rights provided within those civil unions are not always equal to marriage. (How sad that several states in the 2008 election voted against equal rights for gays and lesbians.)

On her radio show Dr. Laura had often spoken so positively about PFLAG and recommended that parents call our national number. I didn't understand her change in attitude. My, things have come a long way since 1995, regarding same sex marriage. Who would have believed that on September 1, 2008, *People* Magazine's cover story would be an exclusive of Ellen DeGeneres' and Portia de Rossi's wedding?

At a second protest against Ms Schlessinger, my sign read: "Gay teens can be hurt by words of Dr. Laura." The quote from *The Dallas Morning News* (9-11-2000) was: "I'm afraid for the teenagers," Ms. Stone said. "Those kids are really fragile when they're coming out. I don't think Dr. Schlessinger is meaning to hurt people. She just doesn't realize the impact she has."

Largely due to these campaigns against Dr. Laura, Paramount Television cancelled her upcoming TV show.

On May 12, 2000, *The Dallas Voice* ran a front page article entitled, "What happens when mom comes out?" by Tammye Nash. It was an interview with three of us moms who came out later in life. The article was in honor of Mother's Day. The cover picture was a colorful one of T.J., Mother, Brad, and myself. The print under the headline said: "3 Dallas women who came out after raising families said honesty only cemented ties with children."

The final media coverage involving my PFLAG work came as a nice cover article in the *Texas Triangle* on July 26, 2002. Dave Gleason and myself were in living color on the front of that issue. The title was "Directing a Decade: Texas PFLAG's unprecedented work and the leadership that's made tomorrow a better place." It was a lovely article by Matt Lum, detailing some of the work Dave and I had done with our local chapter. It also included information about T.J.'s coming out as well as mine. What a great salute from the Texas gay and lesbian community.

I am so proud of all the recognition I received, recognition that honored my affiliation with PFLAG and the gay and lesbian community. However, I am especially proud if I helped distraught parents in some quiet way to better understand and accept their gay and lesbian children. That is really what PFLAG is all about. That is why I saved the following note to share with you at this time; it was in response to my resignation from the Dallas/PFLAG Board. I felt it was time to let go of some of my activities. It read:

"Dear Pat,

Just read a copy of your resignation and I just want you to know how much you have meant to John and me personally. I will never forget the afternoon I called you about PFLAG. You were the first person I ever told that I had a gay son and lesbian daughter. I will always remember our first meeting and how scared we were. With your kindness and compassion and also with Dan's, John and I were soon on our way to becoming supportive parents. We have come a long way since that first meeting, and we owe so much of it to Dan and you. Just know that we will always appreciate what you did for us.

When you made changes in your life, John and I supported you then and support you now. For you to find Evie in your life has been a wonderful thing for you. You know, we think you are so lucky to have first had Dan and now Evie. Speaks well of you." Martha and John England

Chapter 25

On one of my regular visits to my mom, I took her and my step dad some food because Mother had been recovering from a minor bout of shingles. After we ate, the three of us sat around the kitchen table and chatted. I stood up and started to clean away the dishes and casually mentioned that I would load them in the dishwasher. Although Mother had always used her dishwasher in the past, this time she said she would just wash them in the sink. Sam said, "Your mother hasn't used the dishwasher in six months."

There is no way I can adequately explain to you how I felt at that second. It was like something stabbed me in the heart; my stomach quickened, and I wanted to cry. You see, I had read a lot of information on Alzheimer's because it seemed rather prevalent on Dan's side of the family. I knew Mother was sometimes forgetting that I was coming by to pick her up for our outings, but I just told her to keep a note pad handy and write down her appointments. I never dreamed her situation was anything serious like Alzheimer's. She was so youthful, so attractive, so alert. She still did her daily crossword puzzles, and she was faster than any of us in solving the puzzles on "Wheel of Fortune." How could this be? She was 78 years old, and she was the 12th child in her family. None of her siblings had Alzheimer's.

I hoped that I was wrong. On my way home, I bought new books on Alzheimer's. I saw, as I had remembered, that one of the symptoms was no longer using familiar appliances. I now recalled that she had stopped driving;

we all had assumed it was because she and Sam had bought a new car, and she had not yet gotten used to it. She had complained that it had too many new "gadgets." I started to look back and reevaluate her actions; I tried to figure out what was normal aging and what might represent a more serious problem. That was not easy, and I was probably not qualified to take on such a task.

I looked back at our last Christmas, and remembered her giving Brad my dad's police revolver; she also gave T.J. one of her prized family quilts. Brad even remarked at the time, "Mema, you are not planning on going anywhere, are you?" She replied, "You never can tell." I said something about her having a long life ahead of her, that she still had three sisters living – all in their nineties (Her remaining sister recently passed away at the age of 100). I now felt certain that she knew then that something was wrong. How unbelievably sad. What a lonely and scary feeling that must be.

I also recalled that even a year prior, it seemed harder for her to prepare a meal for a family gathering. She sometimes forgot to sit out the silverware or cook the bread, but I hadn't thought much about it. Who doesn't get tired of cooking later on in life? We all just began going out to eat or eating at my place.

I had noticed that she had begun to lose things and often blamed Sam for taking them. Again, I didn't take that too seriously. I saw that she had begun to forget details of my childhood and the sequence of where she had lived. Also, she was becoming more confused and disoriented in places like a medical building, but she had always had a slight problem with that. And who among us have not gotten turned around in a new environment?

I approached Mother about her memory lapses and asked her if she had been concerned about them. She said she had been worried about it. I told her that it could just be normal aging, but perhaps I should take her to a neurologist to make certain. She agreed to go, but she later asked me to cancel the appointment because she had talked Sam into taking her to California to see her sisters and nieces. I worried about their being on the road, but I figured that she felt that it was important to make contact with her family. Sam was 85 at that time, but seemed to be a good driver.

Mother said besides wanting to go to California, she had decided her memory was OK, that she wanted to forget the whole thing. I told her that perhaps her memory was not a serious issue, but I would like to make sure. If it was something serious, we could get her on medication that might prevent or delay further deterioration. I added that I loved her just the way she was, but I wanted her to stay that way. She said she was glad to hear that I loved her the way she was now, and that I could go ahead and reschedule her appointment.

The other shoe dropped for me after that dishwasher incident. I got a call from my cousin in California, a cousin who had never called me in her entire life. Mother had just left from visiting with her and her mom. My cousin asked, "What is wrong with Aunt Martha?" She told me that Mother did not remember that "David" was her (my cousin's) dad. These people were close relatives of my mom's, people she had grown up with and had known very well. In fact, she had continued to visit with them every year, and spoke with them often by phone. It was obvious to them that something was wrong with my mom.

On May 15, 2002, I wrote a letter to her neurologist, sharing with her the symptoms I had seen. I did not want to discuss them in front of my mom. Her appointment was the following week on May 24th. Dr. "Roberts" gave her the basic memory test – asking her the date, the season, who was President, to spell "world" backwards, asked her to fold a piece of paper a certain way and then hand it back to her in her left hand, asked her to write a sentence, gave her three words to remember and to repeat later, etc. Mother did well, only missing a couple of things; she could not remember one of the words, and she was not sure of the season. Dr. Roberts scheduled several additional tests, including a blood test, an MRI, and an EEG. All tests came back showing no physical problems to account for her memory lapses. The doctor diagnosed "probable Alzheimer's" based on those tests, as well as on the memory problems I had described, which also included some personality changes. Dr. Roberts gave her samples of the drug "Aricept" and asked that she return in six weeks. By the way, later I asked Mother what she wrote for her sentence during the test. She said she wrote, "I hope I can do something about my memory." I knew that the doctor could have given her a more difficult test, including reading comprehension, a test that she would not have been able to master. I was happy that at this point she had stuck to the basics. Doing well seemed to give Mother some hope.

Mother had never liked taking medication, and she was even worse now. She would read all the fine print regarding the pills, and then refuse to take them. I begged her to take the Aricept, but she wouldn't budge. I told her that it might help her memory. She said her memory was fine. I told her that she had been diagnosed with probable Alzheimer's; she just looked at me sadly, turned, and walked away from me. I died inside; I hated to use the word "Alzheimer's." but I was desperate. I found out later from one of her neighbors that Mother had confided in her that she had Alzheimer's.

Although I wanted Mother to take the medication, I certainly wasn't going to force the issue. She claimed that my and Sam's persistence in that area was making things worse. She thought her memory was not any worse than that of her friends. So we backed off. It was not as if she was an invalid, someone that we could dupe into taking medication hidden in her food or drink – at least not at that point. I always wanted to treat her with dignity, to not take away any of her rights until and if it was necessary. I never wanted her to feel that I was being bossy toward her. I just couldn't do that, and I would not have wanted to be treated that way by my kids.

In fact, I wrote both my children, letting them know how I felt about the possibility of my coming down with Alzheimer's in the future. I did not want them to take me in their home, that it could destroy their lives and their relationships. I reminded them that I had a long term care insurance policy that would be helpful if I became ill. Hopefully, I will be able to continue paying the premiums, which is looking rather doubtful at this time; it's going up 11% this year. It is my hope that I will be able to take my life if it becomes apparent that Alzheimer's has taken hold of me, unless there has been significant improvement regarding its treatment. Of course, I may change my mind by then, or I might pass the window of opportunity when I would have had the mental ability to do it.

I told my kids that I did not see any major symptoms at that time – only occasional problems with recalling words and names – no major memory lapses or disorientation. My doctor told me that these problems were minor and probably due to stress. I recently saw notes that I had made six years ago about my concern; however, it seems obvious that I have not worsened, so maybe the doctor was right. However, how do we know the length of time the early stages take? I have read that Alzheimer's does not develop quickly for some patients; it might take a decade to get to the point where the signs become more obvious. I know one thing. Don't believe that myth that normal aging means a person loses his keys, and an Alzheimer's patient doesn't know what keys are for. From my experience, that's completely untrue unless you are talking about an Alzheimer's patient in the mid to later stages of the disease. My mom knew exactly what a key was for during her earlier stages of Alzheimer's.

I gave Sam a book on caring for someone with Alzheimer's and asked him to write down symptoms that he saw. One of his notes to me mentioned that she had asked, "Where's Frank?" He was her brother who had died many years ago. Sam mentioned that when he and Mother were leaving the house to go out for breakfast, she had a flashlight in her hand and asked, "Do I need this?" He also related that she often put on her heavy coat to go out, even though it was warm outside. Mother began to rely more and more on Sam and me, always asking us questions on how to do something.

One afternoon I saw that she had a stack of papers on her desk. I went through them, filed some, explained what some of the papers meant, and helped her pay some of her bills. She could still write checks, but it took her a very long time to accomplish the task. As Mother walked me outside to my car that day, she suddenly hugged me and said, "Oh Patsy, thanks so much." It was such a relief to her to get all that paper work put away. She seemed to know something was wrong. When I got home, I was in tears as I related the incident to Evie.

In fact, I shed a lot of tears at night as I lay in bed wondering what would happen to Mother in the future. How could I prepare for that? How could I accept that the time would come that she would no longer know my name or no longer recognize me? Or that she would lose her dignity by not being able to handle bathroom duties or dress herself or feed herself? Why should this healthy, attractive woman, who had such grace and kindness be subject to such a belittling experience? And please don't tell me that God works in mysterious ways. Oh, and there's that lovely, final stage when Mother will become a vegetable – her mind forgetting how to eat and swallow. I guess it's my hope that she will pass away due to "natural" causes like a heart attack or stroke before the long, lingering death approaches.

There were days that Mother seemed "normal." She continued to dress well; she carried on a good conversation with me, and she seemed upbeat. That's the way this horrendous disease lurks within a person, especially in the early stages. It dupes the caregivers into thinking that things are OK, that the person is getting better; then it zaps them in the face with the reality that their loved one is not OK at all; in fact, she is getting worse. The tease was unmerciful, and the roller coaster ride was exhausting. I was reminded of a satellite dish that sometimes picked up reception perfectly; then the clouds came and the reception became distorted.

I began to lose hope, and I had to standby and helplessly watch the mother that I knew slowly disappear. That is so contrary to the human spirit – to accept the fact that things will not improve. My God, something has to be done in the field of Alzheimer's. I continue to read about the new possibilities, but so far there has been no major improvements. I hope ageism is not partly to blame. Perhaps with the "baby boomers" approaching the age of Alzheimer's, we will soon get some real action.

Chapter 26

Evie and I decided to sell the townhouse and move across the street from my mom. Mother was ecstatic! I knew Sam could use my help with her, and I wanted to be able to pop in on them at a moment's notice. I continued taking her out to lunch, as well as going for our regular work out. She seemed more content now riding the stationery bike, rather than walking on the treadmill. One afternoon as we were driving around town, she took her harmonica out of her purse and began to play. I would call out names of various songs (mostly hymns), and she would play them. That gave her a lot of pride; it seemed as if she was showing me that she could still do it. I was truly in the moment with her. We had fun together, but I ached inside – afraid of what the future would bring.

Moving back to my old neighborhood was strange for me – at least for a while. Now I was back living only a few blocks from the house Dan and I shared for twenty years. However, I put away those uncomfortable feelings and concentrated on my mom. I was grateful to be able to check on her so easily. She loved walking across the street to visit with me or to watch me tend to my flowers in the front yard. She often pushed her little dog, Gigi, in a stroller because she had gotten to the point that she could not easily walk due to a hip problem.

It was getting harder for Sam to deal with Mother's condition. She was no longer bathing, and he couldn't coax her into getting in the tub or shower. I have read that some people with Alzheimer's become afraid of water. She lost her concept of night and day, and would often get up in the middle of the night, turn on the lights, and start to work on her puzzle books. She could no longer do crossword puzzles, so I began to buy her those "Find a Word" type of puzzle magazines – the ones where you circle words that are given to you. You have to pick them out of a page of scrambled letters. My friend, Shannon, and I sat many hours with her, all of us working on our puzzle books. Mother loved those times. She also loved it when I came over and sat with her as we listened to her CDs. Music had a magical affect on her. She was able to sing along with the hymns, and she had great fun listening to Johnny Cash. As we listened and absorbed the music, we watched the birds outside her window. This experience taught me a lot about appreciating the basics in life. However, that appreciation did not make up for the fact that Mother's intellect, her personality, her whole being was beginning to disappear.

I was determined to enjoy her and make her life as happy as possible before that happened. Mother tried to oil paint (I had gotten her into painting back in the early 1970s, soon after I started painting.), but it seemed rather difficult for her now. She turned to cutting out pretty pictures from magazines and calendars - then gluing them onto cardboard or canvas boards. Our local art gallery gave her numerous art magazines for that purpose. I was continually buying glue for her, and often Sam and I would pick up frames at garage sales for her work.

She was so proud of her creations. I will always remember one in particular; it was a collection of three photos - that of John Wayne, Martin Luther King, Jr, and Jesus. She wanted her work hung on her walls, and Sam and I nailed them all over her house. I am not exaggerating; they were lined up on every wall, several rows deep! She loved it. I soon got over the fact that this behavior would have not been "normal" for her a few years prior. I let go of the sadness (my sadness) that she would have found this behavior strange when she was my "other mother." Right now she was having fun and she was happy.

Mother was a supporter of President Bill Clinton, and she often sent him money for his library. One afternoon, she asked me if I had seen President Clinton come up on her porch and put something in her mailbox. I said that maybe she had dreamed it. Later when she suggested something like that, it seemed easier and nicer to just go along with her.

I think one of the saddest moments for me personally occurred a few months after we realized Mother had Alzheimer's. She had actually ordered a lovely pink porcelain music box (shaped like a round gift box) for me through the mail; she had written the check for it herself. When she gave it to me, she was afraid it was not nice enough, that the music didn't sound just right. I was so proud of it then, and now I treasure it even more. The title on the bottom says "Always My Daughter," and it says it's a premier issue in "A Mother's Love." When I wind it up, it plays the song, "Always." The music sounds great, but I can rarely listen to it without crying.

Chapter 27

As I mentioned briefly before, I had begun gaining weight again. I'm sure that the stress of Mother's condition, the new relationship with Evie, and the financial concerns played right in to my tendency to eat for emotional reasons. I am not blaming all those factors; I came to the conclusion that I would continue my addiction to sweets whether I was happy, sad, or depressed. That was just the way I was wired, and knowing the causes of my dilemma was not going to create a change in my eating patterns – not long term. For someone who has only 10 or 20 pounds to lose, finding so-called psychological reasons might be of help. For those battling 100 pounds or more, mere psychological discoveries will rarely be the total answer.

Like a lot of people, I gain weight very rapidly. I returned to various methods that I thought I would never try again – the latest diet books and some of the other food programs. They were of no long term help. Then one day after eating alone in one of my favorite Dallas cafeterias, again trying to eat fish and healthy vegetables, I had an epiphany. I stood there and realized that this weight and diet thing was never going to change; it would never get better for me. I would continue dieting, and I would continue to go up and down on the scale. I would continue being depressed from the whole thing, and I would die from the effects of being over weight.

I realized that my discovery of being gay was not the answer to my weight problem. It would have been so neat and tidy for that to have been the entire cause. No such luck. Sure, my childhood had to have played a part in this situation, but so what? Knowing that had not fixed the problem – no matter how much therapy and introspection I subjected myself to.

As I stood there in that cafeteria, I knew that there was only one more answer for me – gastric bypass surgery. At that time, I weighed around 220 pounds, barely enough to qualify for the surgery. From the magazine articles I had read, men usually were required to have at least 100 pounds to lose. Women were sometimes allowed in the programs if they had only 80 pounds to lose. I knew I would be taking a risk, an action of last resort. I knew I could die from the surgery; however, I also knew that it was likely that I would die an early death anyway due to being so overweight. The 220 pounds would soon expand to 230, then 250. Soon I would be back up to my all time high of 265. I seemed helpless to stop it. I was 60 years old, and I felt that the time was right to do this before I got even older and developed a serious illness because of the added weight.

Sure, I hated the fact that I could not follow a sensible eating program, including exercise, and keep the weight off. It sounds so simple; but for many of us, it is not simple at all. I was tired of feeling guilty that I could not succeed at weight loss. I was a very capable person in other areas of my life. It was time to give up on the so called sensible formulas – the ones that only work for most people in the short term. And for those people who can lose massive amounts of weight and keep it off without surgery, I applaud them. However, I know from my research that their numbers are small. Usually most of the weight is regained within two years.

Later that evening I met Evie for dinner at a local pizza place. I mentioned to her that I had come up with a new idea to lose the weight. She sort of laughed and said, "What, surgery?" I told her that she had guessed it. To say the least, she was not pleased. She thought I would be taking too big of a risk. She had always been thin, so she did not understand what I had been going through for 30 years. When she met me, I was also thin – well, let's say I was not overweight. I was temporarily thin due to the Phen-Fen.

Later that night, I explained to Evie in detail my reasons for wanting the surgery; I told her about my past struggles with weight and dieting. I promised to research the procedure and talk to those who have had the surgery performed. Perhaps my insurance would cover it. I wasn't going to go into this without learning as much as possible about the consequences. Evie saw I was very serious about pursuing this, and she began to understand the emotional issues I had been struggling with for many years concerning my weight. She was ready for me to rid myself of the preoccupation with food, dieting, and weight; however, she was still rather concerned for my safety.

I checked out various doctors and hospitals, and received several personal recommendations. The doctor that seemed the best for me was Dr. Dirk Rodriguez; he was head of gastric bypass surgery at Methodist Hospital in Dallas. He had developed a new technique called the "Hand Assisted Laparoscopic Gastric Bypass Surgery." In addition to the small slits, he used a little larger one so that he could get his hand in to guide things – not just relying on the instruments.

By the time I was able to get an appointment to attend a seminar on this method (8-10-2003), I had gained over 10 pounds. Of course I had stopped trying to diet, and as I said, I do gain fast.

I rationalized that the extra weight might help me better qualify for the surgery. I was now at 232, with a BMI (Body Mass Index) of over 40 – an additional prerequisite.

When I talked to Dr. Rodriguez's nurse that day, she was very excited because they had just learned the day before that the American College of Surgeons had asked Dr. Rodriguez to again go there and demonstrate his method while being filmed.

When he looked at my tummy, he said "A piece of cake." He also said the main thing was my safety, and he looked at me very seriously and added: "This will be a major life style change." He also cautioned that this procedure is not to be looked at as cosmetic surgery, but as a way to prolong my life and make me healthier. I learned from the seminar that after surgery, it would be important that I do not over eat or take in too much sugar or fat; if I do, I will get sick (dumping syndrome). It would also be very important that I keep my protein count high, take vitamins, and exercise. So I learned right away that this was not a magic bullet; I had to do my part in order to have a successful long term outcome. The one thing that caught my attention, the thing that I thought would be most helpful to me was the fact that I would no longer be able to binge on sweets without major problems. My affair with candy bars and warm glazed donuts would be over.

Unlike the band surgery you may have heard about, this surgery is more invasive, and I feel it's more effective. Not only is the stomach made smaller, but food will by-pass part of the small intestine. Therefore, fewer calories are absorbed – and fewer nutrients – a major reason for taking extra vitamins. So this is a major surgery that should be discussed at length with one's doctor. Risk and benefits must be seriously weighed. I felt certain it was right for me, but it may not be right for everyone.

First, I had to undergo several medical tests to determine if the surgery would be safe for me. I also had to get a psycho-social evaluation. In addition, I had to send in a doctor's recommendation (with documentation) that I had tried many other alternatives to weight loss, and I had to show any possible physical problems related to being over weight – especially in order to get medical coverage. My cholesterol and blood pressure were rather high, but those alone did not qualify me for coverage. I will never forget the day that I got the call that my insurance would not pay for the surgery. However, they changed their minds a few hours later after receiving the results of my sleep apnea test, which showed I had severe sleep apnea. I had long suspected that something might be wrong with my sleeping pattern. There had been a night that I stayed over with my mom a few years prior, when Sam had been in the hospital. Mother asked me the next morning if there was something wrong, that I had made a choking noise during my sleep. Evie wore ear plugs due to my loud snoring. Now I understood the problem. By the way, I did not tell my mom about the surgery until the day before I went to the hospital. I wasn't sure if she would be able to understand the situation, and I didn't want to cause her unnecessary worry.

I arrived at Methodist Hospital for the surgery on September 24, 2003, weighing in at 244 pounds. Man, as always, I was either gaining weight or losing weight; I looked forward to being able to stabilize my weight – to be able to have clothes of only one size in my closet. I also looked forward to living a longer, healthier life. I breezed through the surgery, and came home on the third day. There were no complications, and I was very grateful. For the first few days, I was on a very soft diet, supplemented with protein powders. I will always remember Dr. Rodriguez saying to me, "If you don't keep your protein count up, you will get sick." Also, he continued his mantra on the importance of exercise in order to keep the weight off.

I was overjoyed by my decision to have the surgery; I felt I had finally found the best solution for my situation. I knew I would have to learn to eat small portions, to eat more often, to emphasize protein, and to eat little fat and sugar. I would also have to exercise and incorporate vitamin supplements into my daily life. From what I had read, I also knew that it would be unlikely that the surgery would be a method for becoming really slim, which was not my goal anyway. However, there was a high probability that I would never venture near that 200 pound mark again.

Chapter 28

I had been home from the hospital about four days when on the morning of October 1, 2003, I heard Evie up early that morning; I was still in bed. I heard our dogs barking and I heard her go out the front door and stay quite a while. I thought she had started preparing our flower beds for the new plants she had planned to install. She often did work like that early in the mornings. I drifted back to sleep. Suddenly she burst into the bedroom, yelling, "Turn on the lights. Turn on the lights. It's bad. It's really bad." I was so scared; I thought she had hurt herself outside, and that she was bleeding. I turned on the light, and she came to my side of the bed and sat down; she was doubled over and crying. She said, "John is dead. John is dead. My son is dead." I said, "No, that can't be." I hugged her in disbelief.

She said that when she was in the kitchen, the doorbell rang, which caused the dogs to bark. She had opened the door to find two Texas Highway Patrol officers on our doorstep.

They explained that John had died around midnight near San Marcus, Texas. Another young man had also died, and alcohol had been a factor. Evie stepped outside with the officers to get away from the barking dogs. She told them she had to sit down. She was afraid she was about to pass out or be sick. The officers gave her a hug and said how sorry they were.

When something like this happens, you can't comprehend it; it doesn't make sense. It's too much to grasp. You say weird things; sometimes you don't know what to say at all. I remember begging Evie to not let this destroy her; she doesn't remember my even saying that. Just as well, because how could it keep from destroying her? I wanted to protect her, but how was that possible? She immediately called her ex-husband, Frank. He had not yet been informed. She then raced out of the house to tell her parents. I hated to see her on the road in her condition, and I asked to go along with her and drive. However, she wanted me to stay home in case there was a phone call with more information. She also wanted me to call some of her close friends.

My God, John was only 24 years old. I began to think back a few years, remembering John's struggle with al- cohol. One evening while he had been visiting Evie and me at our townhouse, she received a call from a police officer who had picked him up for drunk driving. He said he might be making a mistake by not charging him, but the officer let Evie take him home. We talked to John the next morning about the dangers of drinking and driving. Evie told him about a parent's worse nightmare, that he might kill himself and someone else in the process.

He later received similar charges in San Marcus, and he was ordered for treatment. In the summer of 2001, Evie had been able to get him into Hazelden, the treat- ment center I mentioned earlier – the one she had suc- cessfully attended when she was in her twenties. She and Frank visited the center on "Family Day," and tried to be as helpful as possible. John did his 90 days, but thought he could go back to his old neighborhood and hang out with his drinking buddies – and not drink. Unlike Evie, he did not chose to stay in the halfway house near Hazelden and get a job nearby. We worried about him. Evie often talked to him by phone; in fact, she had talked to him the day before he died. They had gotten much closer over the years. She loved him so much.

Evie's parents were devastated by the news of John's death; he was their only grandchild. They were in total disbelief. Evie's mom had spent many nights up late with him, watching movies during his visits at her home. I always saw John at his grandma's and grandad's at Christmas, Thanksgiving, and Easter. Since he was over six feet tall, he usually hung the star at the top of his grandma's Christmas tree. John was a handsome young man - tall, slim, with dark hair and blue eyes; he often brought a girlfriend to the Christmas celebration. He still liked coloring Easter eggs and competing with his cousins to find the plastic ones hidden in the back yard, especially since they usually contained money. How could Evie possibly handle losing him? He had his whole life ahead of him.

To say she was totally devastated by John's death would be an understatement. I could see even during those early days after the accident that part of Evie had died also. I wondered how this would affect her life and our relationship. Even though she feared that this might be how things would end for John, no mother is prepared for it in reality. As we have all heard before, a parent is not supposed to have the burden of burying her child.

Evie threw herself into planning John's funeral; the details seemed to help her get through a horrific time. She chose the music; she designed and printed the bulletins; she decided on various objects that would be on display, like his boots. I collected photos for her and attached them to a display board. She and her ex husband, Frank, worked well together during this terrible time. They had John cremated, and they spread his ashes near the graves of Frank's parents. At the funeral, it was standing room only. So many of John's friends came to pay their respects.

Evie later learned that John's alcohol level at the time of the crash was over three times the legal limit. The bartender who served him, let him leave in that condition. He had been at the bar with his friends. His truck was seen weaving down the highway, and he crashed into the back of a young man stopped at a traffic light.

John was killed instantly, and the other young man never regained consciousness and died hours later. Hopefully, neither felt any pain.

Now Evie had even more guilt regarding John than ever before. It was undeserved guilt; but it was there, deserved or not, and unfortunately it has stayed with her to this day. John was an adult, and Evie had tried many time to reach out to him. I talked her into going to a support group for parents who had lost a child. It was not for her; in fact, she never returned. She absorbed the pain of others; and when added to the pain she already had, it was too much for her. Perhaps, the timing was not right for such a group.

She continued to look back at the years after her divorce and her loss of custody. She wondered if she could have done something differently. I hear that most parents who lose a child, go back and second guess various aspects of their life. Perhaps that's part of the process, but it is very painful to watch. Evie is a "fixer;" that's what she tries to do – whether it's a small problem or a large one. She tried, but couldn't fix John before he died; and she was helpless to fix things now. I wish she did not feel the overwhelming need to repair what is broken. It's an admirable trait, but it causes her much pain and frustration.

I have watched her for years, trying to save the lives of animals that cross her path. She once found a family of tiny squirrels in a nest from a fallen tree; the mother was no where to be found. She brought the squirrels home and fed them with a tiny dropper. She did the same with three newborn, homeless kittens. There was the time that she shook out a tarp, and a hummingbird fell to the ground. It lay lifeless. She immediately scooped it up in her hands and blew life back into it, and it flew away. She must have wanted so badly to do the same for John.

Within a few months of John's death, Evie and I attended a HRC (Human Rights Campaign) event where Judy Shepard spoke about losing her son, Matthew. You may remember his case. Matthew was a 21 year old gay man from Laramie, Wyoming, who was beaten, murdered, and tied to a fence; he died on October 12, 1998. Before Judy's presentation, I introduced myself to her and quickly told her that my partner, Evie, had recently lost her son. Judy turned to Evie and told her how sorry she was for her loss; she added that things would not get better, but they would become "different." When we met Judy Shepard that evening, it had been five years since Matthew's death. Evie has now observed that same amount of time since she lost John.

Even though five years have passed, certain anniversaries are still very hard for her – John's birthday, the date that he died, and Christmas. Then there are triggers from out of nowhere that bring back the raw grief. She says that she has not had that feeling that some parents speak of, the feeling that John has tried to communicate with her. Evie laughs and says that he wasn't a great communicator while he was alive, so she doesn't expect much in that regard. However, she does collect bird feathers that she finds in her path – just in case it's John's way of reaching out to her.

This year Evie has managed to part with some of John's things that she has kept in storage. However, she still has a nice display on her shelf that includes photos, his books, cologne - plus a prized wooden box that contains various mementos, such as his keys, wallet, cell phone, a shirt and his glasses. I will always remember her excitement a few years ago when she discovered by accident that his voice was still in his cell phone memory. I wish I had done a family video during one of the Christmas celebrations so that she would be able to hear his voice.

An additional memento in the wooden box is his watch that she found at the scene of the accident; the time had stopped at the moment of impact. For me, one of the most poignant pieces is his day planner, where he made notes concerning the things he had planned to do.

As one would imagine, losing John has changed Evie. Some of the sparkle has gone out of her eyes, and there is less joy in her soul. She has bouts of depression and anger about the whole situation. It is harder for her to be optimistic about life. However, on the plus side, she has a better set of priorities. She knows how short life can be, and she knows that most of us worry about problems that are rather unimportant.

Chapter 29

Mother's condition continued to worsen. Her ability to sympathize had been affected. It was as if she no longer knew how to show that emotion; perhaps that specific feeling was leaving her completely. Her loss of memory prevented her from dealing with such a situation for longer than a few minutes. Evie and I noticed this when John died. Mother's reaction was limited – nothing like it would have been when she had been "herself." Also, when Gigi, Mother's beloved poodle, died, she cried initially, which broke my heart. However, after Evie and I removed her body from the house, Mother rarely spoke of Gigi at all. A similar reaction happened when Mother's sister passed away. She was very sad at first, but soon forgot it completely.

A startling question came from my mom as we were sitting around my table after Christmas dinner. She looked at T.J. and Brad and asked if they were related. It was very sad for me to hear my son explain to his Mema that he and T.J. were brother and sister. That crystallized what we all knew – that Mother's dementia was progressing rather rapidly. There we all sat, unable to do anything about it. She had been diagnosed with Alzheimer's only a year and a half prior.

A more serious complication soon arose. Mother was becoming violent with Sam, often hitting him with her purse or pushing him. He had hip surgery a few years before, and a hard push could have been disastrous for him. I wanted Mother to be able to stay in her home as long as possible, and I knew that some Alzheimer patients became violent with the family member who watched over them. That was the main reason I did not want to take Mother into my home; it would be more than I could take if she began to attack me. I decided the answer at that time was to bring in an around the clock caregiver to relieve Sam of the pressure he had been under.

That person was a woman named "Malia." Evie and I had met her months before when we were visiting a friend who was recovering from surgery; Malia was her caregiver. She and her little dachshund became part of our family. She, Mother, and I went out to lunch almost every day. We often stopped at garage sales, always looking for frames for Mother's "art work." Malia sat with her for hours, cutting out pictures and helping her glue them into scrapbooks or attaching them to canvases. Incontinence was becoming a problem, but Mother resisted wearing the disposable underwear. Malia and I feared that a major accident would happen while we were out. Mother continued to be very close to me and was always so excited when I pulled up in front of her house to pick her and Malia up for our outings.

The following year (2004), Evie was offered a job she could not refuse in far east Texas. It was at a tree farm where she had worked when she was in her twenties. She loved the area and the salary was very impressive. We certainly needed the money, and I think Evie was ready for a change after losing John. For several months she worked there and came back to Dallas on the weekends. Since it was such a long drive, we decided to move closer to her job location. However, I could not possibly move farther than an hours drive from Mother. I could hardly bare to move at all, but having Malia in place made the difference.

So I sold our house, and Evie and I moved to a lake area about an hour away from Dallas; Evie drove another forty-five minutes to work at the tree farm.

I will never forget the day I drove away from my mom's house as she stood outside waving good-bye to me. She seemed to realize that I was moving away, but I promised her that I would be back at least three days a week to pick her and Malia up for our lunches. I kept that promise, and sometimes Malia drove Mother out to see me.

This arrangement worked for about a year; but as Mother worsened, it became harder for Sam to manage – plus he worried about his son's health. He was battling emphysema, and Sam had already lost one son to the disease. We made the decision that it would be better for Mother and Malia to move near me so that Sam could move in with his son in the Dallas area. Sam would come to see Mother every few weeks. So I sold Mom's house (I was co-owner), and she and Malia moved to a nice, two bedroom duplex about twenty minutes from me. I was so happy to have Mother closer.

The move was rather confusing to her, at least initially. I had hung her paintings on the walls of the duplex and dealt with the movers while Malia had driven Mother around and took her to lunch. When Malia brought her to her new home, Mother kept taking things off the wall, saying they were hers and that she was taking them "home." She seemed happy to see her piano in place, and she noticed her harmonica sitting on the end table next to her blue recliner. Within an hour or so, she seemed perfectly at home.

Soon Malia had her hands full with Mother. It was very difficult to get her to shower or to change her clothes; and I won't even go into the bathroom problems. Mom would get up out of bed several times during the night and wander around the duplex. She would turn on the lights, dust off pictures, wipe the table, go through drawers, etc. We had all doors leading to the outside safely locked; however, one afternoon Mother locked Malia out of the house. She called me, and I was finally able to talk Mother into opening the door. After that episode, Malia always took her keys with her even if she just stepped out back to water the flowers. During the afternoons when Mother became restless, Malia would take her for a drive and get her an ice cream cone.

Mother liked to watch the "Matlock" series on TV. At this time, I wasn't sure how much she understood, but she loved Andy Griffin. When he made his important speech at the end of each show, Mother told us to be quiet and listen. She seemed to think that he could hear us. I tried to find some humor in her behavior in order to get through her stages of progression, but that was very difficult to do.

I soon learned that even though I found each stage very sad, the next stage would be even sadder. I would then look back and realize that what I had found to be so difficult before was nothing compared to what I saw at the present time. I dared to even think what was ahead. This realization made me feel badly for not fully appreciating each stage she was in.

After she was first diagnosed with Alzheimer's, I remembered that next Christmas and how she said that was her "best Christmas ever." That year she loved helping me decorate her Christmas tree by hanging the decorations and talking about specific ornaments. The next Christmas, she hung all ornaments in a clump, not knowing how to distribute them. The following Christmas, she enjoyed watching me hang the ornaments; she did not try to help, but she was very into the process and very complimentary about her tree. The following Christmas, she just sat as I hung the ornaments, not saying anything, not noticing what I was doing, not interested.

Within a year of living with Malia in the duplex, it became clear to us that Mother needed more professional care than one person could give her. She had become violent with Malia, hitting or kicking her when Malia tried to help her with bathroom duties or tried to change her clothes. It was sad to part with Malia, because she had truly become part of my family. I cried when she had to leave us. I wrote a nice letter of recommendation, and we have kept up with one another to this day.

I wasn't ready to put Mother in a nursing home. I felt she was too aware for that, and I wasn't ready to restrict her to only one room of living space. Plus, she would have resisted such a move at that time. I moved her to a lovely assisted living facility that was only about fifteen minutes from my house. Again, I hung all her familiar paintings and made her bedroom and kitchen area look like home. I called to check on her the first night she stayed there. I was told that she was doing fine, that she was sitting in her room in her pajamas, looking through one of her photo albums. I broke down at that image as I related it to Evie. I was afraid she was lonely. How could things have come to this? However, I soon learned that Mother seemed to like her new surroundings really well, and loved the freedom to walk around the facility. Being around other people seemed good for her, and she loved showing off by playing her harmonica. She also entertained everyone by playing the piano in the recreation room.

Of course, the same problems arose there. Mother didn't like to shower, and would tell those assisting her that she "was going to knock their heads off." However, most of the time she was very lovable and kind, and the workers there loved her. Some days when I came to visit, I would find Mother wondering around the dining area, looking puzzled as to where she was. Other times, she would be sitting in the outside garden area enjoying the sunshine. Her face would light up when she saw me approaching. She loved to proudly tell anyone nearby, "This is my daughter!"

She could no longer remember where her room was, and needed assistance to find it. The doctor there put her on a medication for Alzheimer's (Namenda), and it seemed to help a little – at least I hoped it was helping. She still refused to take medication, but they were able to disguise it in milk shakes and other foods.

One afternoon as I was visiting Mother, the aides at the facility were serving her cake in honor of her birthday. We noticed that she was making weird gasping sounds periodically. We walked her to her room, holding each arm. All of a sudden one leg gave out, and she would have fallen to the floor if we had not been holding on to her. The staff thought I should take her to the emergency room at the local hospital. I called Evie, and she met me there. After some tests, the doctor decided that she had been having some TIAs – mini strokes. I later talked to her regular doctor; and he agreed with me that I should consider moving her to the nearby nursing home, that she now needed to be closer to medical care. I remember his words of, "You are now seeing the hand writing on the wall."

So after almost a year at the assisted living facility, I moved Mother to the local nursing home in 2007. I had already researched it, and I was told that it was highly rated. It had been a family run operation for over forty years, and it usually had a waiting list due to its outstanding reputation. I think that sometimes the more reliable and respected nursing homes are often in the smaller towns. Thank goodness, the timing was right to move Mother there. She now needed the added medical attention, and she had passed the stage of resistance. That made it easier on me. I could not have dealt with forcing the issue with her.

Again, I decorated her walls with her oil paintings; however, this time she did not seem to remember painting them. I also hung her framed certificate, showing that she had completed an oil painting course with the famous portrait artist, Dimitri Vail, in Dallas. This was a way for the nurses to get to know Mother, to realize that she had an interesting life before Alzheimer's seized her.

I hung a beautiful framed color photo of Mother that was taken a few years prior, showing hair coiffed and make up in place.

Mother has now lost her desire for lipstick. Until recently she was able to apply it perfectly herself – even without a mirror. The workers at the assisted living facility had to hide her lipstick, because she sometimes drew on the tablecloth with it or decided to "polish her nails" with it. She has always wanted her hair colored, which I have continued. However, I see that may be coming to an end soon, because I am not sure if she notices the difference any longer. But then again, I know she would want it done if she was still "herself." If it becomes a problem for her, I will ask that the beautician at the nursing home no longer do it. That will be a big step for me also; she will no longer look like the mom I have known for years.

Strange as it sounds, I think that since my mom has continued to look like "herself" for these past years, I have been under the delusion that somewhere deep inside her, my mom is still there. I know better, but I want her to be there. She is the only person who has ever loved me unconditionally. I do OK with her situation until I suddenly look back and remember how she was years ago.

A couple of months ago, I walked in to see Mother as she was having lunch in the cafeteria. When she looked up and saw me, she told the nurse, "There's...Patsy." It took her a few seconds to get the word "Patsy" out, but she did it. I had not been sure if she still knew me by name. Every time I enter her room, I announce, "Patsy's here." I want her to remember me, to remember my name. I know it will be hard when I realize for certain that she no longer knows who I am. Frankly, I know that's just around the corner. You know, I have never liked that nickname "Patsy," but coming from my mom's lips, it's just fine.

Mother rarely speaks in full sentences now. She tries to say a few things, but it usually does not make much sense. I sometimes wonder if she knows in her head what she wants to communicate, but she just can't say it. Her walking is very limited, but she seems happy being in her wheel chair. About a year ago, I noticed that she no longer understood how to bend her legs to get into a car.

There are days she can still play her harmonica a little; but usually she doesn't seem to know what to do with it when I put it in her hand. I show her pictures from her albums, but she does not seem interested. She sometimes giggles, which I love to hear, even though I am not sure what brings that response. She rarely makes eye contact with me; but when she does, I am overjoyed. When I play her favorite CDs, she still occasionally claps her hands to the music – especially to Elvis and Hank Williams.

She is more cooperative now with her bath, and she no longer minds the disposable underwear. However, the nurses say if they react too quickly with her, she still hits them. They have learned to talk in very sweet tones, and go slowly with her.

Some days, Mother seems rather alert; other days she stares down at her feet or at her hands. She still enjoys sharing a tiny Hershey bar with me. Until recently, I just handed her the candy, and she would put it into her mouth and eat it; now I break it into small pieces and put them in her mouth. I ask her if it's good, and she says, "Uh hum!"

I notice that the nurses usually have to feed her now, and that her food is often ground up. She must be having trouble chewing, and I'm afraid that is a bad sign. I am told that there will be a day that her mind will cause her to forget how to eat, which involves a complex set of actions. There will be a day that her body will shut down. I hope with all my heart that she does not linger for years in that state.

The literature says that a person may live with Alzheimer's from seven to 20 years. It's now been six years since my mom was diagnosed, and there were probably several years before that when I was unaware of her condition. I dread the day that she will be truly gone, but I look forward to replacing the present memories with those of my mom of years ago. However, that may bring a new and different sadness.

Mother has been at the nursing home about a year. Sam continues to drive the hour to see her every month; he is now 92, and she is 85. My aunt, the one I spoke of earlier (my dad's sister), also continues to visit, even though she lives several hours away. It is very sad for her to see the downhill progression. She has known my mom most of her life and remembers well the other Martha Jo.

I visited Mother on the afternoon of Tuesday, November 4, 2008. Yes, it was election day. I asked her if she loved her "Patsy." She actually responded with "She's the best!" I was not sure if she realized I was Patsy, but I chose to believe she did. I sat close to her and noticed her staring intently at my Barack Obama button that I wore on my shirt. I told her his name and that he would be our next President, and that she would have voted for him, that he was sort of like Martin Luther King (one of her heroes). I doubt that she understood any of that, but it was a good moment. I took her picture with my Obama button pinned to her sweater.

I see Mother at least every other day. I sometimes think I should not go so often, that it would be easier on me and less depressing. However, something pulls me there. It is a bond that I cannot explain, and that I don't fully understand.

Chapter 30

Evie's job at the tree farm did not work out for her; it wasn't a good match. She was better suited to landscaping. Being in an office all day was not a good fit for her. She has become the manager of the landscape company that had originally bought her company years ago. Unfortunately, she still has to drive an hour to work - this time, it's back to Dallas. We decided that the smart thing to do was to sell the house we had bought at the lake area, since it was too large and too expensive for us to now handle.

Since we still loved the area, we bought a smaller, less expensive place about twenty minutes from where we first lived. We are now closer to town (a very small town), and I am only ten minutes from my mom. We were very lucky to have been able to get out from under the burden of the other house before the financial crisis of 2008 hit. We moved to our smaller place in July of 2007, and have been here for over a year now. Evie comes home to the lake on weekends and sometimes once during the week, depending on gas prices.

I love our little place; it's only 1300 sq. ft; but it's on two lots, and the house seems much larger due to the lay out. We made a lot of improvements shortly after we moved in – new paint, carpets, etc. We have two bedrooms, one and a half baths, a large living room, small kitchen, and my sunroom. The front of the house has large windows so that we can see a view of the water and watch the squirrels frolic among our numerous trees. We have an attached garage and a nice back yard for Daisy, Stormy, and Scooter. From my sunroom, I watch the birds, write from my computer, oil paint, watch TV, and play with my dogs. What more could I ask? Well, I could ask for a job, at least a part time job. However, times are hard now, even in small towns. I applied at the local Walmart, and didn't even get a call back! I am currently taking training classes on becoming a substitute teacher. Wish me luck.

I have often wished that I could earn extra money from oil painting, but I have never seriously pursued that. It is difficult to turn art into a profit making endeavor, especially in these challenging economic times. I hope to return to that field, perhaps in conjunction with a part time job. Brenda, my therapist once told me that I "discounted" my painting ability. I had mentioned to her that "anyone could do what I do" - paint with the aid of photographs. She bristled and told me that was not true; she said that if there were ten people sitting in this room, it would be unlikely than any of them could do it. I had always admired the old masters who could truly paint from their mind's eye. However, I have read that the ability to do that is due to the way a person's brain is wired, but it's still a great gift.

A couple of years ago, I worked part time doing general office work for one of the local merchants out here, and last year I did some work for Lory Masters. Remember her? I had mentioned to Lory that I had put all my clippings and articles regarding my work with PFLAG and the gay community into scrapbooks. She said, "Oh, Pat I would pay you a thousand dollars to do that for me!" Since she had worked in non profits for over thirty years, she had boxes and boxes of information she wanted organized. The project turned into 32 albums and many, many hours of work. It was rather overwhelming, but I was happy to do it for her. I was honored that she trusted me with her material. I think that being able to tackle that project and see it to the finish helped inspire me to finally write this book. How fitting that part of the inspiration came from Lory.

I realize that I no longer have the large house I once had or the ability to travel or buy expensive clothes, but I love what I have and I love sharing my life with Evie. My life now reminds me of the Susan Branch card that I have had framed on my desk for over five years: "It's not having what you want that counts, It's wanting what you have." In order to keep what I have, I wish I was better prepared for the job market. I am now 65 years old, which makes that more difficult. But with that magical age, came Medicare and an end to paying the high cost of medical insurance. By the way, I am told that I look more like 55; and I am going to believe it, true or not.

I hate to say that I have regrets concerning my life; but if I am to be honest, I must admit that I do regret not becoming better prepared to support myself financially. As I mentioned earlier, in my day (that terrible phrase), it was common for women to be housewives (also a weird phrase) and to stay home with the children. Perhaps I should have delayed having my kids until I was better prepared to care for them and myself financially – not just relying on that white picket fence to take care of me.

Another alternative would have been to complete my college work and get a job while they were young. Because of my childhood, I was so convinced that I needed to stay at home with them even through their teen years. Who has the luxury to do that anymore? And I am not so sure that the kids raised by a parent staying at home turn out any better than those who have good supervised care from other sources. The mom staying at home may be losing valuable work experience that she may desperately need later. Plus she might achieve a better sense of herself if she was able to contribute to the world at large; the world needs the achievements of all of its citizens.

So I say to the women who feel badly for working while raising their children: "Don't feel guilty. Make special time for your kids. Keep them safe, and take care of yourself financially." I learned this too late. I also commend the older women in our society who balanced their careers with raising their kids, and I respect the women who choose to not have children at all, the women who feel they would rather put more time into a career and other areas of interest. I have obviously widened my view of this situation since I was twenty years old.

I will get off my soap box and move on. It has now been five years since my gastric bypass surgery. You may remember that I weighed 244 at that time; I lost 75 pounds, which put me at 169. That's not skinny, but most people think I weigh in the 150s. Perhaps that's due to my muscle mass. I have kept 70 of that 75 pounds off for five years, which is a miracle for me. As I mentioned earlier, I have always gained or lost weight, never maintained. The surgery has been the answer for me, since I am an emotional eater. I have maintained even with all the emotional issues I have been through – Mother's Alzheimer's, the death of Evie's son, and the financial issues.

I usually wear a size 8 or a 10, which is fine with me. I may try to slowly go on down a few more pounds, but only if I can do it easily – with added exercise. I use my cross trainer twice a day, keeping it in my bedroom where it is easily available. I still pay attention to my protein intake and take those needed vitamins. I have had no discomfort during the five year period as long as I do as I am supposed to – no over eating and take in only small amounts of sugar and fat.

If I eat too much food at one time, my stomach will swell and I become very uncomfortable. I never tend to do that at home, but it's sometimes hard to pay close attention to portion size when eating out. Since my food passes through my system very rapidly, I will become hungry within two to three hours. So it's important that I not grab something that is inappropriate. I have found that at those times, vegetable juice often takes the edge off the hunger until I can work in a protein snack.

I am grateful that I no longer have the extreme cravings for sweets as I had before the surgery. Perhaps that's partly because I know I can no longer handle them in large quantities. However, I still have an occasional candy bar and a small portion of a dessert. I also depend to some extent on good protein bars, the ones with low sugar and fat.

My sleep apnea improved dramatically soon after the surgery, and my cholesterol and blood pressure are completely normal. I feel that I am a much healthier person now – both physically and emotionally.

Evie is very proud of my accomplishment regarding the gastric bypass and my ability to live with the changes it brought. She now agrees that this was the best answer for my situation. I hope there will be a day soon that she and I will be able to be together for more than just the weekends, but that is what works best for us at this time. As the saying goes, "the only constant is change;" so who knows what the future holds.

Even with the emotional upheaval we have faced, we still have a good time together whether it's riding her jet ski, playing with our dogs, going to a dance in Dallas, going to an occasional movie, or lying in bed reading. I am afraid I would feel very lost without Evie, which is a warm, but uncomfortable feeling.

For me, the highlight of moving to the lake area has been the friends I have made here. There are five women in particular who seem like friends I have had all my life; but in reality, I only met them about four years ago. I know how rare that is, and I am very grateful. Usually special friends take years to cultivate, but not with this group. Perhaps that's because we are older, and many of them are retired and have more time for friendships. Perhaps it's because they *make* time for friendships. They are from different backgrounds, but all have originally lived in Dallas. They are former teachers, as well as medical, corporate, and technical workers. Most of them are still active golfers.

We often have lunch together, go to movies, celebrate birthdays, play card games, chat on the phone, go for boat rides, and try to solve the world's problems. We are not in agreement on all political issues, but we still enjoy the discussions. We try to keep in touch with one another; and as we continue to age, that will become even more important.

I met these interesting women through a local non denomination, innerfaith church that serves mainly the gay and lesbian community. I don't classify myself as a religious person; but I certainly try to be a person of ethics. I respect that church, it's minister, and the kind people who attend. I admire the community out reach in which the church is involved, and I look forward to seeing it spread its wings as it moves to its new location. The little church has outgrown its former home, and soon it would have been standing room only.

The words of my mom now come back to me, words from that note she sent me in 1997: "...I want you to know that I will *always* be here for you & my prayers are with you *always*. I know this has not been all that easy for you. Don't think that I haven't seen the pain in your eyes at times. I hope you find a church that you will be comfortable in and meet more friends and become active in helping others." A lot has happened in those eleven years since she wrote that note. I treasure her words; but at the same time, I am exceedingly sad that the note makes such a clear contrast regarding her present mental condition.

I think my mom would be proud that I have achieved the three wishes she had for me. I did find a church where I feel comfortable, and I have meet more friends. I am active in helping others – mainly in Dallas with my Late Bloomer group, and I also speak periodically at various coming out workshops.

Also, I hope by writing this book, I have been of some help to others who may identify with some of my struggles. To write a memoir is rather presumptuous. The writer makes the assumption that she has a story to tell, a story that will touch others. But, you know, we all have a story to tell. Most of us lead rather complicated lives, trying to balance what life throws at us. We reach out for whatever sustains us, whether it's love, friendship, hope, spirituality – the list goes on.

Life is the ultimate mystery, and as the saying goes, "No one gets out alive." So, perhaps the best solution would be to stop badgering ourselves with the questions of "why" (as in "Why does my mom have to struggle with Alzheimer's?") and "what ifs" (as in "What if I had chosen the career route?") and enjoy the short ride out of here, doing what we can to leave a better place behind.

I have really enjoyed this conversation with you, and I hope you feel the same.

3039183

Made in the USA